Prime Numbers Proof and Journey

Finding the Fingerprint of God

Prime Numbers Solved—Mathematical Proof
A First in Twenty-Four Hundred Years

Martin P. Miller, NCARB

WESTBOW
PRESS®
A DIVISION OF THOMAS NELSON
& ZONDERVAN

WestBow Press books may be ordered through booksellers or by contacting:

WestBow Press
A Division of Thomas Nelson & Zondervan
1663 Liberty Drive
Bloomington, IN 47403
www.westbowpress.com
1 (866) 928-1240

Scripture taken from the King James Version of the Bible.

ISBN: 978-1-9736-8209-7 (sc)
ISBN: 978-1-9736-8210-3 (e)

Library of Congress Control Number: 2019920552

Print information available on the last page.

WestBow Press rev. date: 01/30/2020

My Dear Stephanie,

I wrote in memory of you. I had the privilege of visiting your home in the light, but didn't see you. I hope this book conveys my love to your delicate heart. I dedicate the discovery of unit matrix primes to you.

Love Always
PS: Say hi to Euclid, smiles.
—M.M.

Contents

Introduction

Currently the mathematical formula to separate prime numbers from composite numbers is unknown. This book describes how order is discovered in the randomness, by the newly discovered unit matrix primes. Presently, prime numbers are known to be random with no natural logarithm or order to describe the distribution. This book, *Prime Numbers Proof and Journey: Finding the Fingerprint of God*, proves that prime numbers sequence every three rows with unit matrix prime quotients; they provide even distribution; primes are not random and have predictable "white and gray negative spaces" that are composite whole numbers. The math that solves the spacing of primes is simple division with the algorithm of unit matrix primes. Mathematicians working on number theory sought to solve the randomness of prime numbers since Euclid proved that prime numbers were infinite twenty-four hundred years ago.

The prime number sequences discovery occurred when searching for the "fingerprint of God" in numbers. This book explores the fingerprints of God in various topics: the prime number discoveries, near-death experiences, and heavenly visits, all with comparisons and theories.

Chapter 1 discusses the questions why study prime numbers, and did God throw dice placing them. Certainly looks like it—I'd say possibly the work of a three-year-old with randomness everywhere. Why can't we see the order in prime numbers? We know most of nature is very complex. Are prime numbers so complex that man has not figured them out for thousands of years? The Fibonacci sequence is certainly complex as found in nature, trees, galaxies, and shells; which all have a spiral sequence of 0, 1, 1, 2, 3, 5, 8, 13, and so on. The Golden Ratio (1 to 6.18) matches features of the human face and nature. The ancients knew quite a bit about math and numbers. They constructed pyramids all over the world, kept track of farming yields, calculated astronomical positions of planets and stars, understood moon cycles, calculated equinoxes, and much more. In the past three thousand years, the understanding of mathematics has made great strides and has become part of our advancing technology, improving our daily lives.

Chapter 2 discusses God's fingerprint and how to find it and how to seek out hidden ideas. One way to do that is to ask questions and study. We are all capable of finding answers to the unknown and of forging through the unfamiliar. As a young child, I remember wanting to solve the impossible prime number randomness with a table—a table that fifty years later became the answer. What solved the impossible was persistence and time. The number 3 was the fingerprint to look for in solving prime numbers; the find was very significant, and the number 3 is everywhere.

Chapter 3 searches to find order in chaos, rhythm in randomness, and the fingerprints of God. We explore God's fingerprints in nature; in our DNA, in an atom, in a photon, and in the universal language of mathematics, we can find the fingerprint of a creator. Is light just a shining sun, is a feeling just a fading sensation, is it possible to interpret faith without science, or could it be that science has not yet been able to explain the phenomenon of faith? Can thermodynamics describe heaven's energy in a way that predicts a soul?

Chapter 4 is a near-death experience explained with possible scientific solutions: What is the bright light in heaven? How are feelings transmitted? What about something we can feel but not see or touch? Can we travel backward in time and rewrite history? What is a brilliant white floating sphere? What are dreams, and can they tell us anything? Can prime numbers' randomness be similar to life's experiences with an underlying order?

Chapter 5 discusses prime number associations (figure 14), weights, and percentages as they populate in the proof table. Each prime number counts as one unit of weight and then adds columns of brackets of 1,000 cells. There are ten calculation brackets of weights and percentages per column in the 100,000-digit proof table, with four columns of primes ending with the digits of 1, 3, 7, and 9. The original proof was to the first 100,000 digits, and proves by unit matrix primes it extends to infinity. However, this book restructured the proof table to include only the first 2,000 digits. Prime numbers in the new laws form singles, pair primes, or associations/groups (see figure 14). Pair primes have neighboring or adjacent primes combining two prime numbers together. Associations combine pair primes into groups. The largest association, a palindrome, has seven associations or seven pair primes, and all other associations have three pair primes. Singles as seen in figure 15 are the only prime in a row and have no adjacent pair primes or associations in that row. In composing the proof table, the individual cell numbers do not contain a comma separation, for example the number 1623 appears in a cell without a comma. Also, when writing row numbers, they will appear as numerals 1, 2, and 3.

Chapter 6 discusses the singles of prime numbers. Singles are "red" prime numbers with spaces next to them, and singles are the only prime number in the row. The colors are unimportant; you may choose your own for the primes.

Chapter 7 discusses gray spaces or "zees" (figure 16). They are composite numbers, showing a negative space, formed by an algorithm of the unit matrix prime (chapter 7). The unit matrix prime algorithm used to solve this proof resembles the algorithm method used in Euclid's proof written in 300 BC. Interestingly, if Euclid's calculations went a little further, he could have solved prime numbers. Gray space zees whole number quotient are in unit matrix prime column "3," and repeat every third row, which is the fingerprint of the original goal. The proof table calculates unit matrix primes for each column (see appendices F, G H, and I).

Chapter 8 discusses white spaces, which are negative spaces or open space composites derived by an algorithm for unit matrix primes, also the algorithm used in gray spaces. White spaces can never divide by three, because those are the gray spaces. A white space calculates with the proof tables prime number as numerator, divided by the specific column unit matrix prime number as denominator, which produces a whole number or decimal. A whole number quotient is a composite number white or gray space and not a prime number. A decimal quotient or rational number will be a possible prime number.

Chapter 9 includes Miller's laws of primes, which describe the associations, pair primes, singles, and spaces that are in the proof table. Prime numbers sequence every third row, and row 3 holds more possible prime numbers than rows 1 or 2. Row 3 also holds the palindromes, the crown of prime associations, which is all the pair primes—a full house. The goal was to look for 3 as the fingerprint of God, and they are everywhere (figure 6). The first association in the proof table is the super palindrome, which has a 3 in the center of it. The super palindrome are the digits 1, 2, 3, 5, and 7.

Since we're looking for the number 3, or multiples of 3; the super palindrome occurs only once at the beginning of the proof table, and all other combination of 3 such as 33 or 3333 are white spaces because they are composite numbers. The number 1 is a prime number, in this study, because the column of ending digits is also 1, and completes the super palindrome and proof table.

Chapter 1

Searching for Fingerprints—H. G. Hardy

Can We Find Fingerprints from God in Prime Numbers or from Things Around Us?

Searching for the order in prime numbers started with a question: If God made mathematics, did God play dice with prime numbers? They seem random. Einstein didn't think God played dice with the universe when asked about the uncertainty principle; that makes us wonder, perhaps not Einstein, but primes, and sometimes the universe, seem so chaotic. Most of nature is orderly and has entropy, meaning the opposite. Everything starts out orderly but degrades to chaos and even death. Why are prime numbers so different? Mathematics and numbers seem to be the orderly base for everything. Did God pull a switch on us? Nature starts with perfection and goes to chaos? The known laws of physics, chemistry, and biology can all be expressed by orderly numbers at any point in time, and over time matter will degrade by the law of thermodynamics in an open system. If we look at figure 1 closely we can see something, but it's not discerning. Each column has numbers ending in one of two different digits. The first column has ones and sixes; note the primes are only ending in the number 1, and that is true for every column numbers with two or more digits. The single digits seem to stand alone. We can also see a diagonal of groups with a positive slope up and to the right. These are our first hints of order in randomness. Perhaps Einstein is correct.

1	2	3	4	5	6	7	8	9	10	11	12	13	14	15	16	17	18	19	20	21	22	23	24	25
1	**2**	**3**	4	**5**	6	**7**	8	9	10	**11**	12	**13**	14	15	16	**17**	18	**19**	20	21	22	**23**	24	25
26	27	28	**29**	30	**31**	32	33	34	35	36	**37**	38	39	40	**41**	42	**43**	44	45	46	**47**	48	49	50
51	52	**53**	54	55	56	57	58	**59**	60	**61**	62	63	64	65	66	**67**	68	69	70	**71**	72	**73**	74	75
76	77	78	**79**	80	81	82	**83**	84	85	86	87	88	**89**	90	91	92	93	94	95	96	**97**	98	99	100
101	102	**103**	104	105	106	**107**	108	**109**	110	111	112	**113**	114	115	116	117	118	119	120	121	122	123	124	125
126	**127**	128	129	130	**131**	132	133	134	135	136	**137**	138	**139**	140	141	142	143	144	145	146	147	148	**149**	150
151	152	153	154	155	156	**157**	158	159	160	161	162	**163**	164	165	166	**167**	168	169	170	171	172	**173**	174	175
176	177	178	**179**	180	**181**	182	183	184	185	186	187	188	189	190	**191**	192	**193**	194	195	196	**197**	198	**199**	200
201	202	203	204	205	206	207	208	209	210	**211**	212	213	214	215	216	217	218	219	220	221	222	**223**	224	225
226	**227**	228	**229**	230	231	232	**233**	234	235	236	237	238	**239**	240	**241**	242	243	244	245	246	247	248	249	250
251	252	253	254	255	256	**257**	258	259	260	261	262	**263**	264	265	266	267	268	**269**	270	**271**	272	273	274	275
276	**277**	278	279	280	**281**	282	**283**	284	285	286	287	288	289	290	291	292	**293**	294	295	296	297	298	299	300
301	302	303	304	305	306	**307**	308	309	310	**311**	312	**313**	314	315	316	**317**	318	319	320	321	322	323	324	325
326	327	328	329	330	**331**	332	333	334	335	336	**337**	338	339	340	341	342	343	344	345	346	**347**	348	**349**	350
351	352	**353**	354	355	356	357	358	**359**	360	361	362	363	364	365	366	**367**	368	369	370	371	372	**373**	374	375
376	377	378	**379**	380	381	382	**383**	384	385	386	387	388	**389**	390	391	392	393	394	395	396	**397**	398	399	400
401	402	403	404	405	406	407	408	**409**	410	411	412	413	414	415	416	417	418	**419**	420	**421**	422	423	424	425
426	427	428	429	430	**431**	432	**433**	434	435	436	437	438	**439**	440	441	442	**443**	444	445	446	447	448	**449**	450
451	452	453	454	455	456	**457**	458	459	460	**461**	462	**463**	464	465	466	**467**	468	469	470	471	472	473	474	475
476	477	478	479	480	481	482	483	484	485	486	**487**	488	489	490	**491**	492	493	**479**	494	495	496	497	498	**499**	500

Figure 1. Randomness of prime numbers

Choosing the Number 3—Rolling Dice

This is a study of prime numbers, which we've all seen one time or another; after watching a (BBC) movie about them, they seemed different and were not solved for twenty-four hundred years. The movie discussed H. G. Hardy, a famous mathematician who spent his whole life trying to solve the randomness of prime numbers, but they remained random, until now. We all like to design, create, and solve things. Numbers can do these; structural analysis calculates with them; playing games utilize them; rolling dice and moving pieces operate them. The Fibonacci sequence of numbers was discovered and is found throughout nature. Could prime numbers also be part of nature? The randomness of primes seemed to be too complex for a famous mathematician; but follow along, and together we will solve the prime number riddle.

If complexity in nature is from God, could prime numbers be part of this complexity? In searching for the order in prime numbers, a goal requires direction, something that would relate to stories and indications of numbers from God. The impression was that God plays dice with prime numbers. The number 3 is special to the Christian religion, and implies the trinity; my goal would be to find the fingerprint of God and look for the number 3 in prime numbers. Could God have taken any randomness of prime numbers and somehow made them resemble the rhythm of a beating heart or the harmonics of music? If God made Fibonacci numbers the basis for nature, what did he do with prime numbers?

Three is the theme in the crucifixion for Christians and is the fingerprint: in the movie *Heaven Is for Real* (based on a true story), a four-year-old boy visits heaven and points to each palm and each foot when mentioning that Jesus has markers, inferring to the number 3 and crucifixion. Different from the movie *Risen*, where the spikes penetrate the ankles, making four points. The movie *The Passion of Christ* made a good catch when it showed the burial cloth of Christ perfectly wrapping the body, secured by a strip of linen, lying undisturbed in the tomb, with air escaping out of the cloth. And in the movie *Risen* the imprint of the Shroud of Turin was on the burial cloth.

The Shroud of Turin is kept in the royal chapel of the Cathedral of Saint John the Baptist in Turin; it has a strip of linen sewn on one side, which tied the burial cloth around the crucified body. That is how the disciples knew he had risen—the cloth tied with the linen strip was undisturbed, and the cloth collapsed with a faint impression of a face and body on it. The number 3 plays an important part in religion and the crucifixion of Christ. Currently it is factually unknown to science what made the impression of the face and body on the cloth. Increasingly we are discovering past questions through science and archaeology. If a <u>mass transfers to energy</u> (with the calculation of $E=mc^2$), in theory it could become high energy producing surface photons of light. The cloth would deflate from the missing mass that converted to energy; the photons of light from high energy could imprint on a material, producing a brownish impression of the energized body on the surface of the material. This could be one theory for investigation.

Ancient Knowledge—Archeologist Discovery

Prime numbers are an ancient set of knowledge, known throughout history perhaps as long ago as twenty thousand years based on the findings of the Ishango baboon bone tool, recovered at the head of the Nile River. The tool has grooves on it in quantities equal to prime numbers with spaces between, and other sets of grooves on the handle do not have prime numbers. The grooves may only be there to better hold the tool or even be some numeral tracking system. The Rhind 2/n table papyrus from the Egyptian Middle Kingdom about 1650 BC also describes prime numbers as a $ symbol, and the papyrus stopped using the $ symbol after the number 11, indicating they understood Eratosthenes' sieve a thousand years earlier. We have known other equations for over five thousand years, such as the hypotenuse of a right triangle, $a^2+b^2=c^2$ (later a proof called the Pythagorean theorem), used in construction back then. The Pythagorean theorem helps create lengths of 3, 4, and 5 in a right triangle, used to make a perfect square, or 90-degree corner when constructing a building; this is another example of ancients knowing a deeper knowledge of math. However, Euclid, a Greek mathematician born in 325 BC, known as the father of geometry, proved that prime numbers always had one more—they are infinite. Gauss, another mathematician, showed that primes followed a step density graph that flattens out toward infinity. Many more mathematicians have made contributions to primes, but none have shown that they are not random—with predictable separations for primes, and any relation to composite numbers for distribution.

This is a journey to seek out the fingerprint of God in all things around us, including prime numbers, which were investigated, and the result was sequences discovered. We will also explore concepts in quantum physics, and theorize and explain some of the phenomenon we all want to know about. Most of us have heard about near-death experiences; they are becoming too numerous to ignore because these experiences have a consistent narrative—accounts describing bright lights, seeing people that have passed away, observing wonderful vivid colors, visions, health restored, and wonderful feelings.

Is heaven real—the enigma of God—and do the mysteries of heaven create a divergence between science and religion? The ever-increasing technological advances in science agree and disagree with the experiences from heaven. Science is an avenue of change, and religion is a path of unchanging narrative. In the past three hundred years science has diverted from the Bible as history because we don't have the tools to decode our surroundings. Scientists do very well with what they have, and science sometimes conflicts with the Bible currently.

Since geologists postulated the age of the earth in the 1700s, where the great flood could not be discerned, time became a factor of vulcanism and natural processes. Add evolution of Darwin; then add a direct contradiction of the Bible from the excavation of Jericho by archeologist Kathleen Kenyon, and the Bible loses credibility for Exodus. The conclusion from Kenyon and some archeologists is that the Exodus never happened, as there is no evidence of proto-Israelite slaves or a collapse of Egypt during the time of Ramesses. Kenyon correctly dated the destruction of Jericho to the Egyptian Middle Kingdom, and not 1250 BC of Pharaoh Ramesses. It is important to note that the Jericho excavations, including those by Sellin-Watzinger (1907–9), John Garstang (1930s), and Kenyon's (1950s) dating to the Egyptian Middle Kingdom completely match the biblical story in fine detail, excluding Ramesses. Prime numbers such as the history of the Exodus were filled with chaos and randomness, now corrected to an understanding of order that matches the Bible.

The conflict is the Exodus at the time of Ramesses, which is an anachronism. An ancient scribe replaced the location of the proto-Israeli city of the unknown Avaris with the known Egyptian city of Ramesses, creating the chaos today. Documented by Timothy Mahoney in the film *Patterns of Evidence—Exodus*, Mahoney's discovery of the anachronism of Avaris to Ramesses matches the archeology dates for the destruction of Jericho, Hebron, and Hazor by Joshua. More discoveries like this will foster acceptance of the Bible as history. Timothy Mahoney found a fingerprint in history and adjusted our understanding of Exodus to the time of the Egyptian Middle Kingdom, during the time of Pharaoh Dedumes I. This chaos around us is a simple matter of understanding, once we discover the hidden order.

Understanding Primes

We study history to point us in the correct direction—learning and building our knowledge base. Why does anyone study prime numbers, or any numbers for that matter? Like human beings, there are so many, and all are different—not alike at all. Primes have distinctions from other numbers called composites. To understand primes you must know composites; composites are positive integers that have at least one divisor other than one and itself. Composites are the companion to primes and have many factors; the composite number 36 has 3 and 12, 4 and 9, and 6 and 6, while the prime number 31 has itself and one. You might ask, is every positive integer either composite, prime, or the number 1? And the answer is yes. To clarify, an integer is a number such as 1, 5, or 62 and includes 0 and negatives. A prime number is a positive number such as 1, 2, 3, 5, 7, 11, 13, or 331, and its factor is itself and one. Composite numbers are the white and gray spaces in the prime table (figure 6 and appendix A).

Basic to prime numbers are the ability to have only one factor and extend to infinity. The question is do prime numbers have organization—do they have structure, or are prime numbers random? They seem to thin out as we look at them getting larger. We know the primes 1, 2, and 3 are very close together with no gaps in the proof table, but further out, and we find gaps between the primes of 10,069 to 10,079 with three spaces. Even further out 92,507 to 92,551 has a gap of seventeen spaces, and way out we find 982,433,141 to 982,433,143 with no gaps. We can easily see that organization is not present. The question remains with prime numbers, does God throw dice? A prime number used by the magicicada septendecim cicadas has a seventeen-year prime number underground hibernation cycle to evade predators. Prime numbers do have a role in nature—to hide from predators, in this case. We can see in the next paragraph that the proof by Euclid in 300 BC disclosed that primes have an infinite span; there is always one more prime. They seem to be random and haphazard when plotted on a number line, like our human species varied and different. At this point our individual human comparison to primes seems to be stumbling along, unsure of where it is or where it is going. Primes are individual, divisible to one; at this point we have no consistency, as the gaps between the primes vary and have no calculable distance between and no relationships to other numbers, and we start out close but grow further and further apart in a haphazard way. But there is hope; they seem to have a span that goes on forever.

Euclid's Proof—Father of Geometry

Euclid proved that primes always have one more by his computation, and here is how he proved it. Take any consecutive prime numbers, perhaps 2 and 3, add one to the product, and the algorithm gives you a prime. Then add that to the next prime and add 1 again. Let's try it, $2 \times 3 = 6 + 1 = 7$, works because it produces a prime, and again $2 \times 3 \times 6 + 1 = 37$ works again, just by adding 1 we find that adding prime produces more—that is the proof, very simple and solid. Be careful with the algorithm; it is not always correct. Let us take a few more places until we don't find a prime in the equation: $2 \times 3 \times 5 \times 7 \times 11 \times 13 + 1 = 30031$ is not a prime because it has factors other than itself and one.

What Euclid did next was to say that if it does not equal a prime—30031—then it is divisible by a prime not listed in the equation, and will give us new prime numbers not on our list. An example is: 2x3x5x7x11x13+1=30031, which is not prime, so we divide 30031 by a prime not in our equation, and we will find new prime numbers, or its factors 59x509. Both of which are new primes not in our list. In this way we will always find one more prime, or an infinite number of primes.

Gauss's Graph—Prince of Mathematicians

Let us look at prime numbers. They seem to be random with no structure on the right or left of each prime—no consistencies for the number relations—all we know is that we have an infinite number of primes. Euclid just increased our understanding of randomness a lot—to infinity. But a person named Carl Friedrich Gauss, known as the "Prince of Mathematicians," made the next breakthrough in understanding primes. What he did was to draw the primes in a density graph, <u>figure</u>

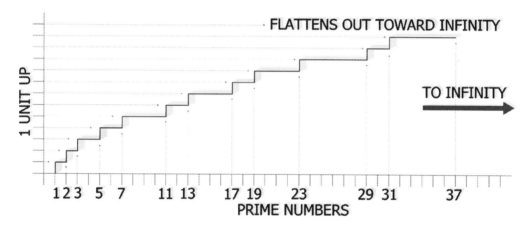

Figure 2. Gauss density graph

<u>2</u>. He did this with a horizontal and vertical step graph, noting each prime number on a horizontal number line starting with zero at the vertex; he marked each point of primes on the number line. At prime 1 on the number line he went up one unit, then to the right to the next prime number, 2. Then he went up one unit and again right to the next prime number, 3, and up one unit, and again right to the next prime number, 5, and up one unit, and again right to the next prime number, 7, and so on. It is a simple concept and produces a stair step effect with longer or shorter various tread lengths, but always increasing the riser by one unit in height.

When compared to individuals, and the real world, this stairway reveals the stairsteps would be hard to navigate; the treads of this staircase are very haphazard and very unsafe even though the risers are always the same height. It seems to fit with the randomness of primes that they have longer, somewhat longer, and shorter, and so on lengths of spacing. Seems we are rolling dice in the length of the treads—not consistent or easy to understand. What Gauss had showed was that the randomness had a pattern; numbers from 1 to 100 have a 1 in 4 chance of getting a prime number; a prime from 1 to 1,000 has a 1 in 6 chance; a prime number from 1 to 10,000 has a 1 in 8 chance. Gauss could not formulate the exact spacing of prime numbers, but he narrowed the randomness, and things look a little brighter. Gauss gave us a stairway up to Euclid's infinity of one more prime.

Fibonacci's Art and Nature

Another interesting group of numbers is the Fibonacci numbers. Leonardo Pisano Bogollo—his real name—lived between 1170 and 1250 in Italy. "Fibonacci" was his nickname, which means "son of Bonacci." He also helped spread the Hindu-Arabic numerals, the digits we use today—0, 1, 2, 3, 4, 5, 6, 7, 8, and 9—which replaced the Roman numerals; that was good or this would be in Roman numerals. The Fibonacci sequence (<u>figure 3</u>) starts at 0 and takes the sum of the two numbers preceding. Let us do an example:

0+1=1, 1+1=2, 1+**2=3, 2+3**=5, 3+5=8, 5+8=13, 8+13=21, 13+21=34, 21+34=55
Result of Fibonacci Sequence: 0, 1, 1, 2, 3, 5, 8, 13, 21, 34, 55, ...

Figure 3. Fibonacci sequence numbers and calculations

The Fibonacci sequence is used throughout nature, whether it be a spiral galaxy, the cross section of sea shells, forks in the branches of trees (the pattern produces the best possible opening for sun or rain on each leaf); sunflower pistils radiate a spiral pattern, flower petals (roses) open in this pattern, leaf veins themselves have this pattern; hurricanes spiral too, and the human face front and sides follow the Fibonacci sequence. The human face is now known to be a product of perfect geometry; we are all beautiful. The variations in the facial Fibonacci make us who we are. The Fibonacci sequence is elegant (<u>figure 4</u>), unlike the primes, which seem to be a disappointment in nature, except for the cicadas. The Fibonacci sequence is obviously not random, but prime numbers seem to be. Or are they?

Figure 4. Fibonacci spiral—boxes add up to adjacent boxes

Each rectangle group forms a golden ratio of:
1 to 1.618

Figure Note: Example 5+3+13=21, 21 is the box to the left.

Also note the rectangle is the Golden Ratio: 13+21=34, and 21+34=55. 55/34=1.618

For over twenty-four hundred years primes have been out of place and upstaged by all other numbers. God did not play dice with the Fibonacci sequence; they provide some of nature's greatest works. And that leads to the golden ratio, which is the number 1.618, and is called the Greek letter phi "Φ," this is calculated by dividing the Fibonacci numbers, which produces something close to these: 13 divided by 8 = 1.625, 21 divided by 13 = 1.615, 55 divided by 34 = 1.618. As you noticed, the larger the numerator and denominator get, the closer to the golden ratio of 1.618. The human face also has these proportions. Leonardo da Vinci and other renaissance painters used the golden ratio proportions in artworks, which are known to be some of the best works ever produced.

Math Is Cold

There is a prevalent preconception that mathematics is cold and unforgiving. Most human recreation includes social activity or individual entertainment such as reading or music. Math in some way is like these activities; in the real world, math works to keep our lives in control—we balance our bank accounts, keep track of quantities, complete rudimentary tasks, count money for purchases every day, play card games, and enjoy music, and we know all activities include mathematical properties. Rarely do we use prime numbers outright; we really do not see them in hidden internet security or used with social media and banking as encryption codes, some 1,234 bits long or longer. Euclid and Gauss showed us that prime numbers are special and that they are infinite and have some order. Could God have put order within the chaos and randomness of prime numbers, giving us a fingerprint? Would God show us randomness and haphazardness with an underlying order that might match the beating of a heart, or the vibrations of music, and even the frequencies of atoms? Do our chaotic lives hold to some underlying order and purpose as we move through the ever-present flow of time?

Chapter 2

Prime Numbers Revealed—Hidden Information

Show Me Your Fingerprint

Prime numbers have been evasive for twenty-four hundred years, yet the answer to randomness is very simple. In elementary school, prime numbers were taught. At ten years old it was hard to understand but intriguing; upon arriving home the problem was a challenge; with a pencil and paper, I started a grid, and numbers were scratched out—could not see anything but disorder in a table of ten columns with prime numbers highlighted. The randomness won; after minutes I gave up. Remarkably, the solution is the same as what was tried fifty years earlier; the only differences are persistence and time. If you have a young child, the child will be able to understand what is in this proof. Let them know they can be very good at video games if they play them often, and math and science are the same. Persistence is knowledge, and studying is the key, per my high school English teacher, Ms. Bertha Tjernagel, a thunderstorm always rumbling. She is gold; her rumbling showed she cared about us, and she brought order to chaos.

The movie about prime numbers in chapter 1 mentioned famous mathematicians and noted that prime numbers were random and unsolved. An internet search found a new mathematical study that reported prime numbers were close to 25 percent random but did not fit the percentages for randomness, and this puzzled mathematicians. With a cup of coffee, my thought was, "Show me your fingerprint, God" on these primes. With paper and pencil, mathematical computations poured out. It took approximately fifty-five hours to solve; struggling through the week, it was taxing.

Solving a Mystery—Persistence and Time

For those of us who lack confidence to accomplish difficult things, we all have the same capacity for learning. Any of us can do impressive things; the requirements are persistence and time. If you do not know it, look it up; if you have a question, ask. In the process for finding the randomness of prime numbers, the method was working long hours each day, focusing with few distractions, taking few breaks, and no lunch. It seems the more you know about a subject, the easier it is to grasp concepts about it. Prime numbers did not reveal their secrets easily; early attempts with various formulas resulted in failed efforts. The randomness was winning. A study table was set up with ten columns of repeating rows and prime numbers added to the table, <u>figure 5</u>. The mystery was that the single digit prime numbers did not fit into columns of 1, 3, 7, and 9; the number 2 did not match anything down below, and the number 5 was just hanging out there.

Kismet—The Number 3

I could not see a pattern or somehow calculate an algorithm that would predict a rule. The single digits were getting in the way every time; the goal was to see the fingerprint of God in these calculations and not the "throwing of dice." Just as I was straining for a solution, I decided to omit the single digits, and kismet. Some quotients dropped into place; just as in Euclid's proof of primes to infinity, not all the calculations worked—only the prime numbers labeled as unit matrix primes, and they only worked with other prime numbers. And seeing God's fingerprint, it all worked out with the number 3, interestingly; see the tables in the <u>appendices</u> for calculations. The gray spaces and prime numbers of <u>palindromes, associations, twins, opposites, and alternates</u> all repeat and occur within the number 3 (<u>figure 6</u>), while the white spaces (composite numbers) repeat from the prime number 7 to infinity. The mathematical sequence of primes revealed itself in the fifty-fifth hour of the investigation. Hidden within the randomness of the primes were <u>unit matrix prime computations</u>, solved with simple division. Gauss, the mathematician who made the prime <u>density graph</u>, would be smiling. With simple division following the new rules for unit matrix primes, negative space locates each prime number position, which are composite numbers that proceed to infinity.

1	2	3	4	5	6	7	8	9	10
11	12	13	14	15	16	17	18	19	20
21	22	23	24	25	26	27	28	29	30
31	32	33	34	35	36	37	38	39	40
41	42	43	44	45	46	47	48	49	50
51	52	53	54	55	56	57	58	59	60
61	62	63	64	65	66	67	68	69	70
71	72	73	74	75	76	77	78	79	80
81	82	83	84	85	86	87	88	89	90
91	92	93	94	95	96	97	98	99	100
101	102	103	104	105	106	107	108	109	110
111	112	113	114	115	116	117	118	119	120
121	122	123	124	125	126	127	128	129	130
131	132	133	134	135	136	137	138	139	140
141	142	143	144	145	146	147	148	149	150
151	152	153	154	155	156	157	158	159	160
161	162	163	164	165	166	167	168	169	170
171	172	173	174	175	176	177	178	179	180
181	182	183	184	185	186	187	188	189	190
191	192	193	194	195	196	197	198	199	200

Figure 5. 10 columns and prime numbers early work

00	X	1 2	3	5 7	&!
0	3	11	13	17	19	&
1	1	21	23	27	29	
2	2	31	33	37	39	2
3	3	41	43	47	49	
4	1	51	53	57	59	1
5	2	61	63	67	69	
6	3	71	73	77	79	&
7	1	81	83	87	89	
8	2	91	93	97	99	2
9	3	101	103	107	109	
10	1	111	113	117	119	
11	2	121	123	127	129	
12	3	131	133	137	139	2
13	1	141	143	147	149	
14	2	151	153	157	159	
15	3	161	163	167	169	
16	1	171	173	177	179	
17	2	181	183	187	189	
18	3	191	193	197	199	&

Figure 6. Prime number proof table looks random with sequences of "3" on the left

The Proof for Prime Numbers

The next six months of investigation developed all the tables in the <u>appendices</u>. The plan was to verify prime number sequences up to fifty thousand digits; that took three months, but during one of my checks an error with a prime in a white space appeared. I thought it cannot be; math is always correct. Then I added another fifty thousand digits for verification, which took another three months, and to my surprise, no errors in that group. It is laughable; what happened was that the prime numbers table I had downloaded initially from the internet was incorrect, by a lot. I found a reputable prime number site and downloaded primes up to one hundred thousand. Within the six months I made new laws for associations, pair primes, singles, verified white spaces, and gray space "zees," with descriptions of white spaces and gray spaces in <u>chapters 7</u> and <u>8</u>. Unit matrix primes, which produce sequences and predictable spaces in primes, are easy to duplicate as follows. A space chosen from the proof table, say 19 divided by a unit matrix prime of 7, produces an answer of 2.714—a decimal and possible prime space. But 189 divided by 7 produces 27, a whole number, which means it will be a white space composite, and not a prime space. It is that easy to predict spaces for primes; they are not random. See the table in <u>chapter 8</u>. I had emailed various mathematicians around the world to spread the discovery of the proof table <u>(figure 6).</u> Perhaps they will make it a complicated set of equations, but it is simple division. I have looked at quantum physics and found the fingerprint number 3, which is the number of particles in the atom—which contains a proton, neutron, and electron.

Chapter 3

Particles of an Atom—Fingerprints Everywhere

Atoms Have Three—More Fingerprints

An atom has a proton, neutron, and electron, equaling three parts. The proton and neutron each encompass 3 quarks and 3 gluons, all prime numbers in figure 7. The periodic table mentions the

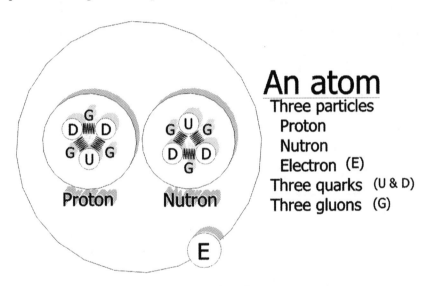

Figure 7 Particles of an atom

atomic mass of each element or atomic number of combined protons and neutrons. Mass is different from weight; weight describes mass with the pull of gravity on it, and the implied description of mass and weight as a solid may not be correct. This is a remnant from the ancient Greeks—the idea of mass as a solid. Some physicists report the atom is energy with no point "solid" mass. Mass is electromagnetic energy in pounds, a unit of measure with no gravity. Keep in mind that electromagnetic fields produce a flux, just like that produced by electric motors, or magnets, and each energizes an area around it. That is how we produce electricity—with magnetic fields moving past a wire. In the atoms the gluons have a strong force, while the proton and neutron have a weak force holding them together. Hydrogen has an atomic mass of 1.007825 u., which converts to a unit of energy. See example in figure 11 for mass to energy conversion $E=mc^2$. I have always presumed atoms to be 100 percent electromagnetic, which implies a spiritual makeup. The body is electromagnetic, held together by electromagnetic forces, and those forces attract and repel other atoms, molecules, and cells. The attraction of electromagnetic forces in atoms is sometimes called "chemical reactions."

DNA—Evolution and Chance

These electromagnetic cells make up our DNA, with long strands that wrap to form 3D structures; these wrapped strands interact on the 3D level—very complex. In the fourth dimension of time the DNA can change to a new level of interaction and protect the body. Is this evolution and chance—that DNA can do this? The atom is the base of DNA. The hydrogen atoms make up approximately 75 percent of the universe. Hydrogen is a base and connects in specific ways to other elements; these elements form molecules and cells, all with the fingerprint of 3.

DNA makes life possible, the Drake equation, which is supposed to explain the number of civilizations in our galaxy, predicted life everywhere back in 1959 with fifty billion civilizations. He corrected this statement and said the possibility was one thousand to one hundred billion. Today's Drake formula includes many of the 1959 ignored concepts for estimating civilizations. One of today's calculations for the equation predicts we are probably alone in our galaxy; other calculations predict a handful, but it all depends on the vast numbers put into the equations. We can see a trend in the calculation for the past sixty years that life is more complex than we ever imagined. In our future calculations, the universe will most likely have us as the only inhabitants. Someone might calculate the chance of the hydrogen atom producing a tree; do not forget to add the Fibonacci design sequence in the tree branches, leaf veins, and roots.

Life—Spontaneous and Time

The Drake equation in <u>figure 8</u> has a set of factors that rely on the supposition that the creation of life is spontaneous through chemical reactions.

$$N = R^* \times fP \times ne \times fl \times fi \times fc \times L$$

N = Number of civilizations in our galaxy which might have a message understood.
R^* = Rate of Star Formations
fP = Percent of stars that have planets
ne = Average number of planets that can support life
fl = Percent of planets that can develop life
fi = Percentage of planets that can develop intelligent life
fc = Percentage of planets that can develop detectable technology
L = Length of time for release of detectable technology into space

Figure 8. Drake equation and factors

Currently, science does not understand the formation of life, and it is beyond our grasp. Life is complex, and the understanding within science to create life is dependent on time and evolution. Within evolution, given each of the animal groups, science has not found a missing link between any of the major animal groups or kinds. The evolution tree, which depicts animals of all kinds with humans on top, shows no missing links between the branches. Could it be that the tree of life is vertical lines of groups or kinds starting and ending the same, with only local changes—changes similar to what we see in dogs over one hundred years of adaption in an environment. What we do not see is a series of small random changes that link various kinds, changing into other kinds in long periods of time, perhaps as long as millions of years, of links of DNA errors to generate ape to man, cow to bear, or dog to horse. We have no compelling cases, but almost all animals start and finish as the same animal for millions of years, with no genetic changes. Keep in mind that we have different families or kinds—cat kinds (Felidae), dog kinds (Canidae), bear kinds (Ursidae), horse kinds (Equidae), and others, which have a gene that allows them to adapt in mutation and evolution of fine-tuning—meaning color changes, longer bird beaks, or changes to adapt to location and the elements, but no evidence for DNA changes into other kinds. Archeology should be one continuous find after another of continuous evolution change. Where are they? Shouldn't they be everywhere? The illustration of Lucy, the missing link between man and ape, was based on 40 percent of the found skeleton in 1974, and the illustrator chose the more human-looking features when drawing the missing bones—misleading and not science. If we sketch the unknown features with "ape" characteristics in the famous illustration, Lucy looks like a typical ape. We have found more fragments of Australopithecus; and Lucy (one of these) is now known not to have walked, because she has curved toes for climbing trees and not walking. The Drake equation depends on one kind turning into another, for which no evidence has ever been found in archeology. And further, the spontaneous transformation of nonlife turning into life, which neither science nor archeology has found. Each decade the Drake equation calculations reduce the chances of finding life in the galaxy because new discoveries from biology, chemistry, and technology put spontaneous life generation toward the impossible. However, it is not these discoveries that will ultimately prove that we are alone or that life is too complex to be spontaneous; but time will disprove evolution and will show a creation from higher energy concentrations.

Time. What Is It, Einstein?

Time's "forces" or cause are currently unknown, and we are searching for the source of the equations that are time. Time is thought of as a flow similar to a stream that moves in one direction. Is it possible that the rhythm of time changes with the expansion of the universe? Is our present perception of time moving slower from the past due to different decay rates of potential and kinetic energy in space? The basic question is if potential and kinetic energy affect space, and entropy is decaying the universe, where did the energies of electromagnetism forming potential and kinetic energy, and matter from decaying space, come from? In chapter 1 we mentioned Einstein didn't correlate God and playing dice with the universe, and specifically the uncertainty principle. Did Einstein want a universe we could understand, with theories that were provable? Einstein didn't like quantum physics in general. The uncertainty principle of particles of waves or points is basically incorrect, I believe. Most physicists would disagree, but they don't know what causes it. We need to question what we are taught and look for supporting evidence in new sources, or your own. Einstein was correct that the particle acts like a point or wave but is not either. What I am surmising is that quantum physics is changing; we no longer have the big bang; string theory is not producing proof; entanglement is not spooky action at a distance; and the uncertainty principle is not uncertain, but all these are natural occurrences (theory for another time, do you see it, look at it in simple concepts). All the natural forces of time, gravity, dark matter, dark energy, entanglement, particles, uncertainty principle, expansion of space, a few unknown particles are all from, and caused, and are part of the same phenomenon (law of new changing physics). I am working on a new book of creation and evolution topics; God's voice or frequency could be the catalyst for particles—a theory for another time.

Relativity and Entropies

The composition of time is unknown by science for both heaven and earth. Descriptions of heavenly time passage often don't correlate with length of earthly time, for near-death experiences. The visit to heaven I experienced did have a sense of time, but I never use an interval of time to describe it. Science tries to explain time through entropy, quantum physics, backwards time travel, relativity, and duplicity, while overlooking philosophy, religion, and history. One theory for the description of time stands out; a physicist named Richard Muller mentions that time is the expansion of space and that the big bang's expansion started time. I find it interesting that in the King James Version of the Bible, Isaiah 40:22, it says God "stretched out the heavens as a curtain, and spreadest them out as a tent to dwell in." This sounds like the red shift we see happening in the universe. The red shift basically tells us that reflected light from almost all distant galaxies is moving—meaning the universe is stretching apart and is moving away from us. Galaxies do have blue shift, but we know those are due to gravity's attraction. (I theorize the expansion is not from the big bang, and today many physicists also agree). Muller uses Einstein's equation of general relativity for flexible and stretchable space-time (see figure 9). With this equation, G=kT, time is relative and may express differences for time in heaven and earth. Another theory for the difference of time between heaven and earth are two entropies: an open energy entropy of our universe and closed energy entropy of heaven. Entropy described in the second law of thermodynamics is for closed systems and is mechanical with no loss; however, an open energy entropy describes the universe. An increase in entropy documents added decay, natural process of past and future, meaning changing time adds decay. And the law also mentions that a closed system has no energy loss, which would lead one to believe heaven is a closed system.

G=kT

Where G is the Einstein tensor, a mathematical description of local curvature and density of space. T is the energy and momentum density of space or energy momentum tensor, and k =2.08 x 10^{-43} expressed in meters, kilograms, and seconds.

Figure 9. Einstein's general relativity equation

Time and Prime Numbers

Time is one of the age-old questions. What causes it? Science has questions and very few answers; scientists are unsure of entropies' role in time, and engineers use it as a law of energy for a closed system. Counter to this is the entropy of an open system as described for our universe's decay. What time is not are pictures or movies, where by observation we calculate the amount of decay from past to future in the pictures. This is the definition of entropy. In this way time is like prime numbers—mysterious with an underlying definition of clockwork, the mechanics of unit matrix primes.

The solving of time is very complex and can be like the inference to prime numbers and entropy. In theory open entropy of time is the continuous decay, has disorder, randomness, and a measurement of change. This describes time on earth, but for heaven the theory for closed entropy fits—the unchanging with no loss of energy. I believe the second law of thermodynamics describes heaven, a closed system with no loss of energy. I theorize that the energy levels are much higher in heaven than on earth based on my experience; it is a closed system, with no loss of energy perceived.

The journey of prime numbers showed us a description of chaos to order, like the energies of earth compared to heaven. Perhaps God hid the order in prime numbers to show that even in randomness and haphazardness, the underlying feature is order with everything having purpose and direction even if we cannot see it or understand it.

Chapter 4

Bright Light and Frequency. Did I Die?

Experience—Light and Peace

The atom being composed of energy with no physical mass leads to a theory; let me explain an experience. One restless night, as I fell asleep, something happened. Suddenly I was in a bright light in a quiet room; an electric white light radiated from the surface of the walls—the kind of white from a television screen with no signal, just pure white, an emanating light. The light did not harm my eyes or overwhelm me but was gentle, and one could even say it was soothing. Two people were in the room with me; they had passed away some years before. I had known them both; one was a war veteran, and both were good people. The room of light had walls, floor, and ceiling. The communication was informational without speech. Things progressed, and at some point my thought was, "I cannot stay here; I have work to do." Then my thought was, "Did I die?" At that moment I felt a weight, perhaps ten pounds, fall away from my body. I no longer cared about the work. My thought turned to this feeling penetrating through me; I could not figure out what it was. The penetrating feeling increased as time passed in the room of light. The thought at the time was, "There is nothing like this down there" (meaning earth). I experienced things and people while in the light; more time passed with visuals, information, and future events, I thought, all happening without speech. Then suddenly, in an instant, I was back in my body. My eyes opened. I tried to remember everything. Was that a dream? It was unbelievably real; the people in the light showed me things—items, events, details transpired. The strong penetrating feeling I had gotten in the light was still with me. "What is that?" I thought. I had tried so many words to fit the feeling, and then the word *peacefulness*—unbelievable peacefulness. It felt as if it was radiating from my body; it was such a strange feeling, that this much peacefulness is possible. It was unfamiliar to me. The peacefulness stayed with me for three days, slowly dissipating from my body, and approximately seventy-two hours later the final emissions left my body; with a soft tug it popped out. My thought was, *Damn, it's gone* (figure 10). Now when people talk about death, and I hear them say they are at peace, I understand.

Is it possible that the feeling stayed with me to confirm that what happened was real? Since then, many other occurrences of wonderful things have happened around me, to reinforce the idea that heaven is very real and that the place of light is an actual place of wonders. Some of these things have happened in various places, with other people present; they acknowledged the events. We know science is always changing, and someday we will know that these miraculous things are possible, one way or another. Undiscovered science is similar to the unknown prime numbers, which were elusive for twenty-four hundred years and were discovered to be simple division unit matrix primes and were easily understood. Science will make discoveries of the miraculous things with simple proof, and in time we will accept them because of science. These miraculous things are undiscovered currently

19

and are not investigated due to fear of labeling. However, quantum physics may describe heaven and its effects on earth; as soon as we learn to investigate the hard truths for science, progress is possible. The second law of thermodynamics can accommodate the exchange of energy, with no physical mass, through a closed system—in theory allowing a soul of pure energy to travel to heaven and allowing the energy from heaven to visit earth. Could it be that the tunnel some have experienced, moving from earth to heaven, is a worm hole? A worm hole in quantum physics is an Einstein-Rosen bridge theory that could link two points in space as a tunnel with an entry point and exit point. Given two vast distances apart, perhaps opposite sides of the universe, the bridge could bend space and make lightspeed travel possible—meaning pure energy with no mass or a soul, could in theory be able to traverse an Einstein-Rosen bridge at the speed of light, traveling across the universe in seconds, or traveling to earth, within the accepted theory of general relativity.

Frequency

In the room of light, the feeling of peacefulness or vibration was very strong and seemed to resonate in my body; we know everything around us on earth has a frequency and vibrates; this would be true for heaven also. The higher energy in heaven is the reason near death experiences have reported brighter colors, whiter lights, no time connection, no decay, and no open entropy; heaven would be a closed system with no energy loss. It is important to note that entropy can exchange energy like the vibration of feelings but not matter with the external environment. In theory energy (feelings) can export from heaven and be experienced on earth. When I woke up, the very strong feeling of peacefulness dissipated at the square of the distance x, "the loss of feeling," which looks like a smooth curve (<u>figure 10</u>). The feeling fading diagram starts out very strong at the top of the graph and dissipates toward the vertex on day three, down and right. Upon my return, the frequency of peacefulness dissolved, seemingly into the surrounding atmosphere, meaning the higher energy decays to the lower energy surroundings, quickly at first and then slowing—like heat, higher energy radiating to the surrounding cool air as entropy. We know frequencies in the universe are in an open

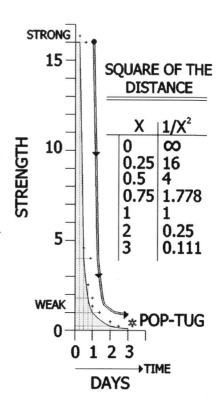

Figure 10 Square DistanceTable Feel

system of entropy and decay. While in heaven, where walls radiate light, the higher energy vibrations or frequencies show presence of a closed system, where energy remains with no loss.

Photons—Wall of Light

Quantum physics can describe the wall of radiating bright light with quantum electrodynamics, a.k.a. QED. Physicists describe and theorize about photons of light, which are particles that have electromagnetic charge. When high-energy electrons move to a lower state, they give up their extra energy in the form of a photon of light. From the room and place of light I was in, does this show high energy in heaven, where walls radiate photons of light? Is this a description of the room of light? Energy, frequency, and wavelength are related with the Planck-Einstein relation, also known as Plank's relation (figure 11). We can calculate the amount of energy in electron volts (eV) of a green photon of 2.2556 eV, which converts to mass with $E=mc^2$, and the actual mass $= E/c^2 = 2.2556/299792400^2 = 2.503 \times 10^{-17}$ kg.—a small number that moves the decimal place over to the left seventeen spaces. What we have done is show that a photon of light has energy (voltage), and frequency (vibration): **E = 2.255 eV and v = 5,4545 x 10^{14}.**

Photon Equations (energy to mass conversion):
Equation: The energy of a photon: $E = h(v) = h(s/\lambda)$.

Units
Given: Where: E=Energy [J, Joules or eV, electron volt], λ = wavelength [m, meter], and v = frequency [Hz., Hertz] = c/λ.
c = Velocity of Light 2.997×10^8 ms; h = Plank's Constant 6.626×10^{-34}; λ = Wavelength; v = Frequency; 1 eV = 1.602^{-19} J
Given: 550×10^9 m $= \lambda$

Example calculation of a photon of green visible light λ = 550 nm
v = Find Frequency c/λ = $(2.997 \times 10^8$ ms$)/(550 \times 10^9$ m$)$; =; v = **5,4545 x 10^{14} s^{-1}[Hz.]** This is the frequency of one green photon
Energy = $(6.626 \times 10^{-34}$ Js$)(5,4545 \times 10^{14}$ s$)$; = ; 3.614×10^{-19} J
(or **2.255 eV**) This is the energy of one green photon
Mass = E/c^2 = 2.255 eV/$(3.0 \times 10^8$ ms$)^2$= 2.503×10^{-17} kg

---

Figure 11. Example: the energy and frequency of one green photon of light

QED—Backward Time Positron

QED also predicts backward time with the appearance of a positron smashing into an electron and the appearance of a photon. What the description of a positron smashing into the electron has done is give the appearance that backward time travel is possible, because the positron appears out of a photon, before the collision with the electron (figure 12). The experiment views nature in the relationship of space and time and how it interacts with electrons and photons. Let us describe the experiment; we have a photon of light A moving toward an electron B, both moving up through time; before they meet, the photon A splits into two, creating an electron C and a positron D. The positron D keeps moving up through time toward the electron B, and when they collide they annihilate each other and produce a photon E, and the photon E continues in the direction the electron B

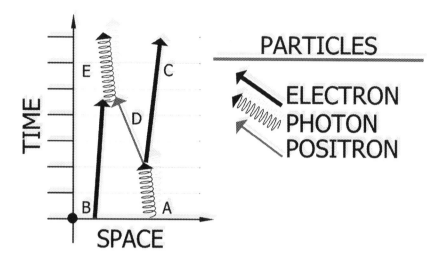

Figure 12. Example of electron and photon interactions

was traveling. This split before the collision noted in QED (quantum electrodynamics) theory notes this as backward time—curious, is it natural to have backward time? We have a photon A and electron B switch places later in time in the QED description and produce Photon E and electron C. In <u>figure 12</u> the diagram is a theory conceived by Richard P. Feynman and describes the interactions of a photon and electron—a strange theory of light and matter. Note the electrons and photons in the diagram. Could this be a "similar" situation within the room of light, where an electron releases a photon. Science calls these particles a duplicity, because in certain tests they act either like a wave or a particle. I believe it is neither. (I will leave the new description of what it is to you, and a discussion for another time.). Physicists noted that this is not backwards time, with no convincing theory.

Near-death experiences have described people in heaven as when they died or as they appeared in their earlier years. The obvious correlation is that backward time travel is responsible for a person appearing younger; however, I do not believe this is the case. Backward time travel is not possible as stated in <u>figure 12</u>. The positron D is not splitting in time before it reaches electron B due to backward time as suggested by Richard Feynman. In theory heaven and a person's age is entropy in a closed system, where energy remains and can reinitialize to an earlier state or later state in theory. Thus healing, eyesight, and age may take the form of any state in a closed system of very high energy. What was matter on earth stayed on earth and the converted energy may enter heaven per the law of thermodynamics. What controls heavenly entropy is unknown. Is it as simple as gases and liquids in a closed bottle where matter never escapes. Shaking the bottle of gas and liquid produces a new state, and later the bottle returns to the original state of liquid and gas, with no energy loss inside the closed bottle system. The bottle can absorb heat from the outside as energy or radiate heat from the bottle as an energy exchange, with no loss of matter in the bottle and no mass exchanged. Metamorphically the high-energy heavenly particles may change to various configurations without loss of energy.

Glowing Spheres—Electromagnetic Shell

Glowing spheres, some bright white and others gray or muted, have been described as speeding through the air. Once I had viewed a bright white sphere approximately six inches in diameter. I yelled over to the other person in the room, "Rachel… look… here." She saw the glowing sphere. The sphere, stationary, wanted to see us, or wanted us to see it; as it took a position straight in front of me, it was very close, and I could see fine details on the sphere. The other person excitedly said, "Take a picture." I had a new camera out of the box and looked down to figure out how to take a picture and missed its departure. The other person said it "made an *S* trajectory and left." The person also said it was "very bright." I asked for more detail later, and the departure movement was described like a backward *S* with curved swipes, and it went up through the ceiling into the adjacent space. When I first saw the sphere up close, it was mostly transparent with small cylinders covering it—each clear with a slight glow and no colors but only see-through white light. The cylinders attached to the sphere were very small and covered the whole sphere evenly. The sphere may have been an electromagnetic shell in theory, producing photons of light. Possibly it was "intelligent," because it was stationary and then moved away all in an orderly fashion, and it was very beautiful. In a closed system of entropy, it is important to note that entropy can exchange energy but not matter with the external environment.

The question is are we seeing an energy exchange from a closed system? Time (day or night) is not a factor in the appearances. The very bright light mentioned in the sphere's departure reminded me of the walls of light. That day of the sphere, other things had happened that night that involved the number 3, including four other numbers in sequence. I had seen the large sphere only once. I give these examples so that science may investigate, even construct and review, shells of photonic energy and the compositions they may take. What were the small glowing cylinders on the shell?

Premonitions and Science—Uncover the Truth

Premonitions and dreams from the light show love or concern always; they predict the future or an idea. Premonitions describe real life experiences; if you have one, you will wake instantly at the end. The problem is that you do not have a timeframe to put them in; they may happen days, months, or a lifetime later. One experience of a premonition was a dream for three consecutive days, each showing a little more of a black truck quickly pulling into my driveway and then quickly backing out. The third time my eyes were straining at what was happening as the truck pulled in. I could not understand what the truck was doing in my driveway. In the dream I was sitting viewing a security camera tablet; the truck pulled in "fast-forward" then backed out "fast-forward." While straining my eyes and bending forward in the dream, to get a better look, my eyes suddenly opened, and I was awake watching the dream in front of me, which seemed to be projecting on the wall. A few days later my security camera caught a black truck pulling into my driveway, a man getting out and going behind the house—happened in less than two minutes—and it was burglarized. The burglary happened when I was selling my home. I had two appointments back to back. My real estate person told me it would be best to stay away for the two showings. For some reason, I was uneasy and stopped home between showings and looked at the security camera. Recorded was the black truck driving in, a thin white male with a baseball cap getting out and walking to the back of the house for seventy seconds. He emerged back into camera view, got back into his truck, backed out, and was gone, all in about ninety seconds—or per my dream fast-forward.

In reviewing the tablet, earlier by about twenty minutes, the security camera showed a man (who worked at the military base) and his wife setting up the home for the burglary. The wife cornered an old crippled real estate salesperson in the bathroom while the man went downstairs into the garage/ basement and unlocked the back door. A few minutes later the man came up from the garage and emerged at the vestibule and went out the front door. After the front door closed, it slammed, and the wife moved from the bathroom door, letting the crippled real estate woman out of the bathroom. The man, now outside, walked into the middle of the street and took off his baseball cap and then replaced and removed it a few times. He stayed in the middle of the street for about thirty seconds looking toward one end of the block and then got into his car and sat there. The wife and real estate woman emerged outside a few minutes later. Could it be that taking off the baseball cap in the middle of the street was a signal that the house was set up for the black truck burglary?

Here is a twist. I had decided to be at the house for the rest of the showings, until the home sold. The next day a young girl made a last-minute appointment to look at the home, and to my surprise, she was driving the black truck. I replayed the security camera, held the tablet to the window and identified the black truck as the same one from the day before, identical with a one-of-a-kind marking. The young girl, it turned out, was the wife of a military intelligence man who owned the black truck. (Note: the man who unlocked the back door was from the military base's MI also). I went outside and copied the plate number of the black truck; later, I told a government undercover person who lived across the street what happened. He investigated and said they were military intelligence, and the black truck burglar had a history of this before being in the military. My neighbor also mentioned when he entered the license plate number to search for the owner, the machine lit up like the fourth of July. Which means he was part of our law enforcers. Dreams do come true.

In the premonitions, communication is vital—a voice you do not recognize will tell you things; the voice is always unfamiliar and is sometimes gentle, sometimes stern, fitting the occasion. Sometimes the premonition happens when you're awake; sometimes you are above looking at yourself and the surroundings. The premonitions are in color, and some have sounds such as explosions or flashes of light, while others have no sound. Words are usually concise; spoken words are clear and understood (except once). The words used have a deep understanding, and sometimes physical effects stay with you when waking. One voice of reason in a dream has confounded me for twenty years; the discussion told me something. He must have thought I was intelligent because I couldn't understand his phraseology. After thinking for a few minutes, the Phraseology had the aura or inference of forgiveness, I could not understand? Most of the words I did not know or were vaguely familiar. Waking premonitions are perceived as a TV screen in front of you; they are shown quickly, lasting only seconds, and again fast-forward. The premonition (dream) of the truck had no words or other indicators—just the dream of the truck pulling in and out quickly, and looking at a tablet. The premonition did not indicate any words such as "burglary between showings" making the premonition easier to decipher. In this case the dream materialized, fact, the security recording was copied on a CD, and police were called, no report made.

I have a very practical construction and scientific view of things. I need hard facts, and I do know heaven is real. What I have learned is that if we cannot explain it with science, it does not mean it is not credible; it just means science has not caught up with what we know as faith. Be skeptical and research; if you do not know it, look it up. If you have a question, ask. Remember that the Bible's Exodus story lost credibility, with most archeologists stating the exodus never happened. And now with the film by Timothy Mahoney, the exodus happened and took place in the Middle Kingdom of Egypt. Science is catching up, like the prime numbers' randomness and chaos, hiding the reality of sequences and order. Science needs to keep an open mind and research all areas and uncover the truth.

Science Changes Every Day

Remember not long ago some believed that the earth was flat. The following are examples of our changing science: In 1877 Mercury's wobbly orbit was thought to be caused by a nearby small planet or moon, as theorized by Le Verrier; he called this hypothetical planet Vulcan. With this, many amateur astronomers around Europe, eager to be part of a scientific discovery, claimed to have witnessed the mysterious planet Vulcan. Another mistake was made by Aristotle, who believed inanimate matter like slime or mud made life spontaneously from nothing—based on his own observations of maggots seemingly generating from dead animals. This idea was believed until the 1700s. Also, philosophers as far back as the Greeks believed that light required a delivery system called luminiferous Aether, and this was believed through the 1700s. Also, in error at the turn of the twentieth century was the theory that the universe was static and unchanging. Albert Einstein calculated a static universe into the theory of general relativity, which he considered his "biggest blunder." Seems Albert Einstein changed his calculation to match "current views" of a static universe. Opposed to this is Einstein's widely accepted theory of relativity that wasn't accepted in the scientific community for many years after it was introduced. Our research must take account of tough and unpopular questions and process the hard truth, no matter how impractical it may seem to science at the time. We have both creation and evolution in our investigations. We will make mistakes; it is what we do. Look at creation and evolution as two investigations. Keep in mind that science always changes. The Bible narratives never change (scribe errors).

If You Could See God, Would that Make a Difference?

We question God, with the randomness and chaos as part of this world; we ask why things don't go our way. He created us in his image after all. When you know God is present and around everything, is the interaction with God different? Then it is with just faith. What if you had seen the face of the Father (I Am) and Jesus? If the Father looked very much like us, would that make a difference? Would your faith be stronger? If I said the Father was nice looking, perhaps tall, broad shouldered, big boned/medium build, no facial hair, very dark short hair parted on the right, strong deep voice, medium-small nose, walked/ran with purpose, and was very confident, would that make a difference? If I said Jesus was nice looking, medium dark hair with highlights parted in the center, tall, medium nose long/little drop, medium-to-thin build, cropped beard, tender voice, and blue-green eyes, would that make a difference?

Randomness—Finding Order

Our prime numbers have a fingerprint of the number 3, have order, are predictable with unit matrices, and shed light on the discovery for negative space composites—the haphazard space between primes (figure 13). This is an entertaining journey with descriptions of science and mathematics—finding the order in prime numbers while looking for the fingerprint of God in the prime number 3. Quantum physics explains why the walls in the room of light radiate photons, why colors are brighter, why we have no time correlations to earth in heaven, and why we have no decay; the reality is that heaven exists as a place of higher energy in the closed system of entropy. We find the order in prime numbers by unit matrix primes in figure 13. Given the prime column on the left, in the columns of 1s, and the unit primes in the row at the top. When we divide the left prime by the top unit prime, we get a whole number, or rational number. If the quotient is a whole number (shown by a box in the table, except the number 1) we find gray and white spaces between the prime numbers. If we take any gray or white box whole number and move it to the column, we get a space and not a prime number. If "all" the divisions calculated in a row with a single prime divided by the unit primes are decimal or rational numbers, the column number will be a prime number.

Beautiful Things and Numbers

The Fibonacci sequence and prime numbers describe everything around us; they reveal the complexities of a spiral galaxy or the constant rhythm of a beating heart, put chaos to order, and show predictability in negative space, like the unit matrix primes have done (figure 13). Mathematics solves the questions of our universe, whether philosophical or physical. It describes who we are and what we do. Prime numbers moved into a category of understanding and familiarity, they are now in a graceful category with the Fibonacci sequence of beautiful things and numbers. Prime numbers can resemble the normal heartbeat rhythm shown as unit matrix primes, the dispersion patterns of gravity, light, and heat, the harmonics of music, or the frequencies of atoms. Prime numbers are mechanical in and underlying logic of structure, organizational process, and scheme. While the Fibonacci sequences are art, together they describe man, machine, everything in science, and the heavens.

#			2	3	5	7	11	13	17	19	23	29	31	37	41
0	3	11	5.5	3.666	2.2	1.571	1	0.846	0.647	0.578	0.478	0.379	0.354	0.297	0.268
1	1	21	10.5	7	4.2	3	1.909	1.615	1.235	1.105	0.913	0.724	0.677	0.567	0.512
2	2	31	15.5	10.333	6.2	4.428	2.818	2.384	1.823	1.631	1.347	1.068	1	0.837	0.756
3	3	41	20.5	13.666	8.2	5.857	3.727	3.153	2.411	2.157	1.782	1.413	1.322	1.108	1
4	1	51	25.5	17	10.2	7.285	4.636	3.923	3	2.684	2.217	1.758	1.645	1.378	1.243
5	2	61	30.5	20.333	12.2	8.714	5.545	4.692	3.588	3.21	2.652	2.103	1.967	1.648	1.487
6	3	71	35.5	23.666	14.2	10.142	6.454	5.461	4.176	3.736	3.086	2.448	2.29	1.918	1.731
7	1	81	40.5	27	16.2	11.571	7.363	6.23	4.764	4.263	3.521	2.793	2.612	2.189	1.975
8	2	91	45.5	30.333	18.2	13	8.272	7	5.352	4.789	3.956	3.137	2.935	2.459	2.219
9	3	101	50.5	33.666	20.2	14.428	9.181	7.769	5.941	5.315	4.391	3.482	3.258	2.729	2.463
10	1	111	55.5	37	22.2	15.857	10.09	8.538	6.529	5.842	4.826	3.827	3.58	3	2.707
11	2	121	60.5	40.333	24.2	17.285	11	9.307	7.117	6.368	5.26	4.172	3.903	3.27	2.951
12	3	131	65.5	43.666	26.2	18.714	11.909	10.076	7.705	6.894	5.695	4.517	4.225	3.54	3.195
13	1	141	70.5	47	28.2	20.142	12.818	10.846	8.294	7.421	6.13	4.862	4.548	3.81	3.439
14	2	151	75.5	50.333	30.2	21.571	13.727	11.615	8.882	7.947	6.565	5.206	4.87	4.081	3.682
15	3	161	80.5	53.666	32.2	23	14.636	12.384	9.47	8.473	7	5.551	5.193	4.351	3.926
16	1	171	85.5	57	34.2	24.428	15.545	13.153	10.058	9	7.434	5.896	5.516	4.621	4.17
17	2	181	90.5	60.333	36.2	25.857	16.454	13.923	10.647	9.526	7.869	6.241	5.838	4.891	4.414
18	3	191	95.5	63.666	38.2	27.285	17.363	14.692	11.235	10.052	8.304	6.586	6.161	5.162	4.658

Figure 13. Unit matrix primes sequenced by unit primes.
(See appendix F for space tables.)

God's Interest

The complexity of our world can be represented by mathematical formulas, whether it be the Fibonacci sequence or steady rhythm of the sequences describing unit matrix (prime number) columns. It seems an inevitable comparison that the chaos and randomness of prime numbers is similar to life's experiences—we never know what to expect. But is it possible that underneath our trek through life, we have an underlying path that is orderly and known by God. Our experiences on earth, if following primes' nature, are a catalyst for an eternal arrangement of order and peacefulness.

The following chapters describe the prime numbers proof, with supporting documents in appendixes A through J.

Chapter 5

Prime Numbers Associations and Percentages

Prime numbers are seemingly random and are associated into singles or pairings of adjacent prime numbers into the following:

			1		3		7		9			
Super palindrome	00	X	1	2	3	5	7				&!	Single digit primes associations
Palindrome	0	3	11		13		17		19		&	4 in a row association
Twins removed	15	3	161		163		167		169			Centered cells associations
Opposites	39	3	401		403		407		409			Outside cell associations
Twins left	27	3	281		283		287		289			Left cell associations
Twins Right	33	3	341		343		347		349			Right cell association
Split left	2	2	31		33		37		39			Left cell omits center association
Split right	1	1	21		23		27		29			Right cell omits center association
Single prime	99	3	1001		1003		1007		1009		1	Single cell omits other cells

Figure 14. Associations, pair primes, and singles

The named colored cells have the following properties in this book: the reference to blue or brown tones are shown as black cells with a white number; and occupy row 3. The reference to magenta is shown as a gray cell, with a white number; and occupies row 1. The reference to green is shown as a gray cell, with a black number; and occupies row 2. The reference to a red single is shown a as gray cell, with a black underlined number. The gray zees are shown as an "X" in the cell. And, the white spaces are shown as white cells, with black numbers.

In the percentages and weights of table 1 below, the colored titles are the pair primes. The **Primaries** above with PR on the left side in each colored column, and are the major row or row where most of these pair primes occur. **Alternate** pair primes occur in row 3, only for splits and singles, and are alternates because they occur less often in row 3 than in rows 1 and 2. The blue and brown pair primes occur only in row 3 and never in row 1 or 2. The super palindrome only occurs once in row X and is composed of single digit prime numbers. I started with row X because the single primes do not fit into any group except super palindrome.

The percentages and weights in the table below show Alternates and Primaries of pair primes as they occur in column groups of approximately one thousand. See underline{appendix A}: Proof of Prime Numbers to 100,000 for the statistical data.

Weight per thousand rows, per column (larger percent data bars have more prime number occurances)

AL = ALTERNATE OR LESS ROW PRIME #3
PR = PRIMARY OR MORE PRIME ROWS IN #1 OR #2

Note: single digits not counted (row 00).

Table of prime number occurrences in rows 1, 3, 7, & 9 per thousand digits and percentages of occurrence in brackets

PALINDROMES ROW 3		TWINS REMOVED ROW 3		OPPOSITES ROW 3		TWINS LEFT ROW 3		TWINS RIGHT ROW 3		SPLIT LEFT ROW 2, ALT 3		SPLIT RIGHT ROW 1, ALT 3		ROW START	END
AL	PR	AL	PR	AL	PR	AL	PR	AL	PR	AL	PR	AL	PR		
0	37	0	422	0	405	0	401	0	407	421	823	383	796	TOTALS	
	1.101%		7.007%		6.507%		6.707%		6.306%	6.807%	13.614%	6.406%	13.814%	Percent of	999
	11		70		65		67		63	68	136	64	138	1	
	0.701%		4.605%		5.305%		4.905%		4.404%	4.905%	9.510%	4.404%	9.409%	Percent of	1,999
	7		46		53		49		44	49	95	44	94	1,000	
	0.300%		4.304%		3.303%		4.204%		4.404%	4.304%	7.808%	4.104%	8.709%	Percent of	2,999
	3		43		33		42		44	43	78	41	87	2,000	
	0.200%		4.004%		4.004%		4.505%		3.904%	3.804%	7.107%	3.904%	9.109%	Percent of	3,999
	2		40		40		45		39	38	71	39	91	3,000	
	0.100%		4.304%		3.604%		3.604%		3.904%	3.804%	8.008%	4.204%	7.307%	Percent of	4,999
	1		43		36		36		39	38	80	42	73	4,000	
	0.200%		3.504%		3.504%		3.904%		3.203%	3.303%	6.206%	3.704%	7.407%	Percent of	5,999
	2		35		35		39		32	33	62	37	74	5,000	
	0.300%		3.804%		3.403%		2.402%		3.504%	4.204%	7.107%	2.703%	5.305%	Percent of	6,999
	3		38		34		24		35	42	71	27	53	6,000	
	0.300%		3.604%		3.804%		3.403%		3.203%	3.403%	7.307%	3.103%	6.406%	Percent of	7,999
	3		36		38		34		32	34	73	31	64	7,000	
	0.300%		3.704%		3.403%		3.303%		3.504%	3.704%	7.508%	3.003%	6.206%	% PER	8,999
	3		37		34		33		35	37	75	30	62	Percent of 8,000	
	0.200%		3.403%		3.704%		3.203%		4.404%	3.904%	8.208%	2.803%	6.006%	Percent of	9,999
	2		34		37		32		44	39	82	28	60	9,000	

Column digits contain odd whole numbers

The occurrences of prime numbers reduce as we approach infinity

Table 1. Percentages and weights

Chapter 6

Red Single Primes—Doing the Random Shuffle

Red singles are the prime numbers alone in a row that have no pair primes or associations with them in a row, and singles occur in any row; however, like split rights and split lefts, the majority are in the primary row, which are rows 1 and 2. And the alternate row is row 3, where singles occur less than in either of the primary rows. The following is a description of the singles as they appear in the proof. Each red single is 1 unit in weight, per column section, with a total of all singles in each column in the underline proof table.

			1	3	7	9		
SINGLES LEFT-RED ROW 2	17	2	*181*	183	187	189		PRIMARY ONE IN ROW 2 (WEIGHT OF 1)
SINGLE MIDDLE LEFT-RED ROW 1	10	1	111	*113*	117	119		PRIMARY ONE IN ROW 1
SINGLE MIDDLE RIGHT-RED ROW 2	8	2	91	93	*97*	99		PRIMARY ONE IN ROW 2
SINGLE RIGHT-RED ROW 1	13	1	141	143	147	*149*		PRIMARY ONE IN ROW 1
ALTERNATES - ROW 3 ONLY	-	3	*OR*	*OR*	*OR*	*OR*	3	ALTERNATES ARE IN ROW 3 ONLY
SINGLE LEFT ALTERNATE - RED ROW 3 ONLY	180	3	*1811*	1813	1817	1819	2	ALTERNATE ROW 3, PRIMARY # NOTED AT END
SINGLE LEFT MIDDLE ALTERNATE - RED ROW 3 ONLY	204	3	2051	*2053*	2057	2059	1	ALTERNATE ROW 3, PRIMARY # NOTED AT END
SINGLE RIGHT MIDDLE ALTERNATE - RED ROW 3 ONLY	54	3	551	553	*557*	559	2	ALTERNATE ROW 3, PRIMARY # NOTED AT END
SINGLE RIGHT ALTERNATE - RED ROW 3 ONLY	99	3	1001	1003	1007	*1009*	1	ALTERNATE ROW 3, PRIMARY # NOTED AT END

Figure 15. Red single prime numbers—primaries and alternates

See appendix C Red Singles Calculations for percentages, weights, and location in the table of red singles.

Chapter 7

Gray Spaces—A Fingerprint

Gray spaces are very mathematical, called "zees" because to the Z pattern they produce when calculated. The calculation of the proof table prime number divided by unit matrix prime produces a number space in the Table 2A through 2D of primes below; if it produces a whole number (a number without decimal places) it is a gray space (when divided by 3). If it produces a decimal of 0.333 or 0.667 it is a possible prime number space. The following tables show how to calculate a gray space. Figure 16 shows the relationships they form to each other in the prime table rows 1 and 2.

UNIT MATRIX PRIME GRAY SPACES CALCULATION MATRIX - TYPICAL FOR ALL ROWS 1 - 2 - 3

EXAMPLE $\dfrac{21}{3} = 7.000$ If a prime ending in "ONE" is divided by unit prime 3 it will produce a decimal of the following:	SEE "UNIT MATRIX PRIME WHITE SPACE MATRIX" COLUMN 1, FOR WHITE SPACES STARTING AT PRIME UNIT 7 THE SEQUENCE IS THE UNIT MATRIX PRIME NUMERATOR	LINES	ROWS	COLUMN 1	UNIT Calculations 3
Row 1 will produce a decimal of n.000 (ZEE Gray Space). Whole number is a space.		1	1	⊠	7.000
Row 2 will produce a decimal of n.333. Decimal is not a space - possible prime.		2	2	31	10.33333333
Row 3 will produce a decimal of n.667. Decimal is not a space - possible prime.		3	3	41	13.66666667

Table 2A. Unit matrix prime gray column 1

UNIT MATRIX PRIME GRAY SPACES CALCULATION MATRIX - TYPICAL FOR ALL ROWS 1 - 2 - 3

EXAMPLE $\dfrac{33}{3} = 11.000$ SEE "UNIT MATRIX PRIME WHITE SPACE MATRIX" COLUMN 3, FOR WHITE SPACES STARTING AT PRIME UNIT 7 THE SEQUENCE IS THE UNIT MATRIX PRIME NUMERATOR If a prime ending in "THREE" is divided by unit prime 3 it will produce a decimal of the following:		L I N E S	R O W S	C O L U M N 3	3
Row 1 will produce a decimal of n.667. Decimal is not a space - possible prime.		1	1	23	7.66666667
Row 2 will produce a decimal of n.000. (ZEE Gray Space). Whole number is a space.		2	2	33	11.000
Row 3 will produce a decimal of n.333. Decimal is not a space - possible prime		3	3	43	14.33333333

Table 2B. Unit matrix prime gray column 3

UNIT MATRIX PRIME GRAY SPACES CALCULATION MATRIX - TYPICAL FOR ALL ROWS 1 - 2 - 3

EXAMPLE $\dfrac{27}{3} = 9.000$ SEE "UNIT MATRIX PRIME WHITE SPACE MATRIX" COLUMN 7, FOR WHITE SPACES STARTING AT PRIME UNIT 7 THE SEQUENCE IS THE UNIT MATRIX PRIME NUMERATOR If a prime ending in "SEVEN" is divided by unit prime 3 it will produce a decimal of the following:		L I N E S	R O W S	C O L U M N 7	UNIT Calculations 3
Row 1 will produce a decimal of n.000 (ZEE Gray Space). Whole number is a space.		1	1	27	9.000
Row 2 will produce a decimal of n.333. Decimal is not a space - possible prime.		2	2	37	12.33333333
Row 3 will produce a decimal of n.667. Decimal is not a space - possible prime.		3	3	47	15.66666667

Table 2C. Unit matrix prime gray column 7

UNIT MATRIX PRIME GRAY SPACES CALCULATION MATRIX - TYPICAL FOR ALL ROWS 1 - 2 - 3

EXAMPLE $\dfrac{39}{3}$ = 13.000 If a prime ending in "NINE" is divided by unit prime 3 it will produce a decimal of the following:	SEE "UNIT MATRIX PRIME WHITE SPACE MATRIX" COLUMN 9, FOR WHITE SPACES STARTING AT PRIME UNIT 7 THE SEQUENCE IS THE UNIT MATRIX PRIME NUMERATOR	LINES	ROWS	COLUMN 9	UNIT Calculations 3
Row 1 will produce a decimal of n.667. Decimal is not a space - possible prime.		1	1	29	9.66666667
Row 2 will produce a decimal of n.000. (ZEE Gray Space). Whole number is a space.		2	2	39	13.000
Row 3 will produce a decimal of n.333. Decimal is not a space - possible prime		3	3	49	16.33333333

Table 2D. Unit matrix prime gray column 9

LINE	ROW	COLUMN 1	COLUMN 2	COLUMN 3	COLUMN 4	ALTERNATE
1	1	21	23	27	29	
2	2	31	33	37	39	
3	3	41	43	47	49	
4	1	51	53	57	59	
5	2	61	63	67	69	
6	3	71	73	77	79	

Figure 16. Typical gray space configuration "Zees"

Chapter 8

White Spaces Are Predictable—Gauss Smiles

White spaces are very mathematical; the calculation of white space prime numbers is simply the prime number divided by unit matrix prime, which produces a number in the unit matrix prime white space matrix of spaces, if it produces a whole number (a number without decimal places) it is a white space. White spaces vary in location in table 7; however, they are very predictable in the unit matrix. The unit matrix is based on columns of prime numbers to infinity. Unit matrix primes columns spaces repeat every time the unit matrix prime or denominator is "counted down" in sequence. The following figure 17 shows how to calculate a white space.

See the following Appendices for White Spaces Unit matrix prime Calculation Matrices Data:

Appendix E: White Spaces Calculated
Appendix F: Unit Matrix Prime White Space Matrix Column 1
Appendix G: Unit Matrix Prime White Space Matrix Column 3
Appendix H: Unit Matrix Prime White Space Matrix Column 7
Appendix I: Unit Matrix Prime White Space Matrix Column 9

Calculation example: Prime number 169 in the proof table divides by the unit matrix prime number 13, shown in the heading of the table, and produces a quotient of 13. White spaces shall continue every 13 spaces in this column. Just as the column of unit 7 prime number shows that the interval of seven cells produces a white space in the unit matrix prime white space matrix tables and proof table, keep in mind a quotient that of 1 will automatically be a prime number.

UNIT PRIME WHITE SPACE MATRIX: COLUMN 9 WHOLE NUMBERS OTHER THAN ONE ARE SPACES

EXAMPLE: *TABLE CELL 169 ÷ BY UNIT CELL 13 = 13*

LINES	ROWS	COLUMN 9	UNIT 2 COL 9 NO SPACES (NO WHITE SPACES) 2	UNIT 3 COL 9 GRAY SPACES REPEATS DOWN EVERY 3	UNIT 5 COL 9 NO SPACES (NO WHITE SPACES) 5	UNIT 7 COL 9 WHITE SPACES REPEATS DOWN EVERY 7	UNIT 11 COL 9 WHITE SPACES REPEATS DOWN EVERY 11	UNIT 13 COL 9 WHITE SPACES REPEATS DOWN EVERY 13	UNIT 17 COL 9 WHITE SPACES REPEATS DOWN EVERY 17	UNIT 19 COL 9 WHITE SPACES REPEATS DOWN EVERY 19	UNIT 23 COL 9 WHITE SPACES REPEATS DOWN EVERY 23	UNIT 29 COL 9 WHITE SPACES REPEATS DOWN EVERY 29
0	3	19	9.5	6.333	3.8	2.714	1.727	1.461	1.117	1	0.826	0.655
1	1	29	14.5	9.666	5.8	4.142	2.636	2.23	1.7	1.526	1.26	1
2	2	39	19.5	13	7.8	5.571	3.545	3	2.294	2.052	1.695	1.344
3	3	49	24.5	16.333	9.8	7	4.454	3.769	2.882	2.578	2.13	1.689
4	1	59	29.5	19.666	11.8	8.428	5.363	4.538	3.47	3.105	2.565	2.034
5	2	69	34.5	23	13.8	9.857	6.272	5.307	4.058	3.631	3	2.379
6	3	79	39.5	26.333	15.8	11.285	7.181	6.076	4.647	4.157	3.434	2.724
7	1	89	44.5	29.666	17.8	12.714	8.09	6.846	5.235	4.684	3.869	3.068
8	2	99	49.5	33	19.8	14.142	9	7.615	5.823	5.21	4.304	3.413
9	3	109	54.5	36.333	21.8	15.571	9.909	8.384	6.411	5.736	4.739	3.758
10	1	119	59.5	39.666	23.8	17	10.818	9.153	7	6.263	5.173	4.103
11	2	129	64.5	43	25.8	18.428	11.727	9.923	7.588	6.789	5.608	4.448
12	3	139	69.5	46.333	27.8	19.857	12.636	10.692	8.176	7.315	6.043	4.793
13	1	149	74.5 (RED)	49.666	29.8	21.285	13.545	11.461	8.764	7.842	6.478	5.137
14	2	159	79.5	53	31.8	22.714	14.454	12.230	9.352	8.368	6.913	5.482
15	3	169	84.5	56.333	33.8	24.142	15.363	13	9.941	8.894	7.347	5.827
16	1	179	89.5	59.666	35.8	25.571	16.272	13.769	10.529	9.421	7.782	6.172
17	2	189	94.5	63	37.8	27	17.181	14.538	11.117	9.947	8.217	6.517
18	3	199	99.5	66.333	39.8	28.428	18.09	15.307	11.705	10.473	8.652	6.862
19	1	209	104.5	69.666	41.8	29.857	19	16.076	12.294	11	9.086	7.206
20	2	219	109.5	73	43.8	31.285	19.909	16.846	12.882	11.526	9.521	7.551
21	3	229	114.5	76.333	45.8	32.714	20.818	17.615	13.47	12.052	9.956	7.896
22	1	239	119.5	79.666	47.8	34.142	21.727	18.384	14.058	12.578	10.391	8.241

Annotations in figure: GRAY SPACE; RED; WHITE SPACE (13); WHITE SPACE; INTERVAL; PRIME # =1 (1); WHOLE NUMBER WHITE SPACE (EXCEPT #1) (27)

Figure 17 Unit Matrix Prime White Space Calc diagram

Chapter 9

Miller Laws—Prime Numbers

Line	Row	Col.	Col.	Col.	Col.	Alt.
00	X	1	3	7	9	

No.	Laws	Example Columns & Descriptions					

No. | **Laws** | **Example Columns & Descriptions**

1

Sequenced With 1, 2 & 3; Repeating "1, 2 & 3" To Infinity.

00	X
0	3
1	1
2	2
3	3

To **Infinity**

Prime numbers sequence every third row to infinity. They are not random, and have predictable spaces.

The table start with an **X** indicating a non- row for single digit primes. The next, row starts with double digits at **3**. Then, sequences repeat to **infinity**.

2

"Super" Palindrome

Row X (Law 1) Has the Only Single Digit Prime Numbers.

00	X	1	2	3	5	7		&!

The ampersand designates a palindrome. The exclamation indicates the super palindrome.

Note: "color" designations are in the book gray scale

Super Palindrome (navy blue) happens once in prime numbers and consists of single digits: 1, 2, 3, 5, & 7 at row X. Number 1 is a prime, such that column 1 incorporates primes ending in digit one.

3

Palindromes

0	3	11	13	17	19	&

Palindromes (cyan-blue) appear across columns 1, 3, 7 & 9 a total of 37 times at lines: 0, 9, 18, 81, 147, 186, 207, 324, 345, 564, 942, 1299, 1563, 1572, 1605, 1803, 1890, 1941, 2100, 2226, 2529, 3171, 3483, 4377, 5133, 5532, 6297, 6720, 6948, 7221, 7725, 7968, 8103, 8271, 8880, 9783, 9912.

Palindromes appear only in row 3, and have no alternates

| Twins Removed | 15 | 3 | 161 | 163 | 167 | 169 | |

4 Twins removed (blue) appear in columns 3 & 7, and only in row 3. They have no alternates.

| Opposites | 39 | 3 | 401 | 403 | 407 | 409 | |

5 Opposites (blue) appear in columns 1 & 9, and only in row 3. They have no alternates.

| Twins Left | 27 | 3 | 281 | 283 | 287 | 289 | |

6 Twins left (tan-blue) appear in columns 1 & 3, and only in row 3. They have no alternates.

| Twins Right | 33 | 3 | 341 | 343 | 347 | 349 | |

7 Twins right (brown-blue) appear in columns 7 & 9, and only in row 3. They have no alternates.

Twins Primes Appear Only in Row 3	15	3	161	163	167	169	
	27	3	281	283	287	289	
	33	3	341	343	347	349	

8 Twin primes appear only in row 3 as primary, never row 1 or 2. Twins have no alternates.

Diagonals not mapped, such as 283 to 347, or 163 to 281.

Vertical Twins	2	2	31	33	37	39	
	3	3	41	43	47	49	2
	36	3	371	373	377	379	1
	`37	1	381	383	387	389	

9 Vertical twins can occur in columns 1 and 7 in rows 2 and 3. Also in columns 3 and 9 in rows 3 and 1 only.

10 — Triples do not form.

1	n		Prime		
2	n		Prime		
3	n		Prime		

Triples never occur vertically in any of the columns. Because unit matrix primes cannot be prime and sequence every third row.

11 — Split Left

2	2	31	33	37	39	

Split left (magenta) appear in columns 1 & 7 in row 2 as primary, and row 3 with less weight as an alternate.

Weight = quantity of occurrences in a column selected.

12 — Split Right

1	1	21	23	27	29	

Split right (green) appear in columns 3 & 9 in row 1 as primary, and row 3 with less weight as an alternate.

13 — Alternate Split Primes

24	3	251	253	257	259	2
36	3	371	373	377	379	1

Alternate (magenta and green) prime numbers can occupy row 3. The primary split left (green) are in row 1 (Law 11). The primary split right (magenta) are in row 2 (Law 12).   (This law does not include single red alternates)

14 — Row 3 (And X) Associations

00	X	1 2	3	5 7		&!
0	3	11	13	17	19	&
15	3	161	163	167	169	
27	3	281	283	287	289	
33	3	341	343	347	349	
39	3	401	403	407	409	
24	3	251	253	257	259	2
36	3	371	373	377	379	1
57	3	581	583	587	589	2
132	3	1331	1333	1337	1339	

Row X occupies a Super Palindrome.

Row 3 may occupy a grouping of any palindromes, twins, opposites, splits, a single, or be open. Note Row 3 contains alternates for only split magenta and split green, otherwise blues and browns are primary in row 3.

15

Row 3 – all possible associations

9	3	101	103	107	109	&
3	3	41	43	47	49	2
21	3	221	223	227	229	1
12	3	131	133	137	139	2
6	3	71	73	77	79	1

Row 3 may occupy: seven associations as a palindrome. Associations of threes as twins and splits, or opposites and splits.

Note: twin browns not exposed in the row and are present underneath the primes shown, and each counted as weight.

16

Splits never combine in row 1 or 2, with other primes

4	1	51	53	57	59	
5	2	61	63	67	69	

Right split can only occupy row 1 in columns 3 & 9. Left split can only occupy columns 1 & 7.

(omitted gray "X" spaces for clarity)

17

Single primes

99	n	*OR*	*OR*	*OR*	*OR*	

If a single (red) prime is in a row then no other prime can occupy the row. Only one single per row, with three empty spaces.

18

Single left

17	2	*181*	183	187	189	

Single left (red) appears in column 1, row 2 as primary. And row 3 with less weight as an alternate.

19

Single middle left

10	1	111	*113*	117	119	

Single middle left (red) appears in column 3, in row 1 as primary. And row 3 with less weight as an alternate.

	Single middle right	8	2	91	93	97	99

20

Single middle right (red) appears in column 7, in row 2 as primary. And row 3 with less weight as an alternate.

	Single right	13	1	141	143	147	149	

21

Single right (red) appears in column 9, in row 1 as primary. And row 3 with less weight as an alternate.

	Single alternate primes	99	3	OR	OR	OR	OR	1

22

Single (red) alternates will always be in row 3. The primary singles row is 1 or 2. And #1 in the box at the end of the row indicates the primary row. See law 18 through 21.

	Single left alternate	180	3	1811	1813	1817	1819	2

23

Single left alternate (red) appears in column 1, in row 3 as an alternate. Note the primary row 2 at the end of the row in the red box.

	Single middle left alternate	204	3	2051	2053	2057	2059	1

24

Single middle left alternate (red) appears in column 3, in row 3 as an alternate. Note the primary row 1 at the end of the row in the red box.

	Single middle right alternate	54	3	551	553	557	559	2

25

Single middle right alternate (red) appears in column 7, in row 3 as an alternate. Note the primary row 2 at the end of the row in the red box.

Single right alternate	99	3	1001	1003	1007	*1009*	1

26

Single right alternate (red) appears in column 9, in row 3 as an alternate. Note the primary row 1 at the end of the row in the black box.

Gray space "zees"	1	1	21	23	27	29	
	2	2	31	33	37	39	
	3	3	41	43	47	49	
	4	1	51	53	57	59	
	5	2	61	63	67	69	

27

Gray spaces or "zees" are non-prime spaces that occurs in rows 1 & 2. Primes cannot occupy (gray) spaces.

Prime number colors omitted for clarity.

Gray spaces are the same as white spaces except the spacing is every third row. See "unit matrix prime gray spaces calculation matrix" for details.

White spaces	9989	2	99901	99903	99907	99909	
	9990	3	99911	99913	99917	99919	
	9991	1	99921	99923	99927	99929	
	9992	2	99931	99933	99937	99939	
	9993	3	99941	99943	99947	99949	
	9994	1	99951	99953	99957	99959	
	9995	2	99961	99963	99967	99969	
	9996	3	99971	99973	99977	99979	2
	9997	1	99981	99983	99987	99989	
	9998	2	99991	99993	99997	99999	

28

White spaces are non-prime spaces that occur at intervals of the "unit matrix prime white space matrix" for columns 1, 3, 7 & 9.

Prime numbers can never occupy a white space.

Calculate spaces by dividing the prime number by the unit matrix prime. The resulting rational and whole numbers that are a sequence of the unit matrix prime; such that a unit matrix of 7 will produce a quotient whole number (or white space) every seventh cell.

See "unit matrix prime white space matrix " for details. Four matrices provided for columns 1, 3, 7 & 9.

29

White space groups increase to infinity

UNIT MATRIX PRIMES INCREASE WITH

PRECEDING ROW PRIME TO INFINITY

			Gray	White	White…
LINES	ROWS	COLUMN 9	UNIT 2 COL 9 SPACES	UNIT 3 COL 9 GRAY SPACES (TENS)	UNIT 5 COL 9 SPACES
			NO WHITE SPACES	REPEATS DOWN EVERY	NO WHITE SPACES
			2	3 1	5
0	3	19	9.5	6.3333 2	3.8
1	1	29	14.5	9.6667 3	5.8
2	2	39	19.5	13 1	7.8
3	3	49	24.5	16.333 2	9.8
4	1	59	29.5	19.667 3	11.8
5	2	69	34.5	23 1	13.8
6	3	79	39.5	26.333 2	15.8

Rows and columns to infinity

See "unit matrix prime white space matrix " for details. Matrices provided for columns 1, 3, 7 & 9.

30

All primes sequence every three rows

Blue primes are in row 3.

Green row 1

Magenta row 2

Alternates row 3

00	X	1 2	3	5 7		&!
0	3	11	13	17	19	&
15	3	161	163	167	169	
27	3	281	283	287	289	
33	3	341	343	347	349	
39	3	401	403	407	409	
24	3	251	253	257	259	2
36	3	371	373	377	379	1
57	3	581	583	587	589	2
132	3	1331	1333	1337	1339	

All primes must obey the rules of sequenced primes. Base on unit matrix prime whole number, and rational number calculations.

Table 3 Miller Laws for Prime Numbers

Appendix A

Proof Prime Numbers to 2,000

(Table is to two-thousand digits or two-hundred rows. Request an
original proof of one-hundred-thousand from the author)

(Proof Table 4)

PRIME NUMBERS PROOF OF SEQUENCES								
DESCRIPTIONS	LINES	ROWS	**COLUMNS**					ALT.
30 NEW LAWS								
PREDICTABLE TO INFINITY								
SEQUENCED								
NOT RANDOM			1	3	7	9		
Super palindrome: single digits	00	X	1 2	3	5 7			&!
Palindrome: seven associations row 3 only	0	3	11	13	17	19		&
Split right: primary row 1	1	1	21	23	27	29		
Split left: primary row 2	2	2	31	33	37	39		
Twins removed; twins left: & Split left: alternate 2	3	3	41	43	47	49		2
Split right: primary row 1	4	1	51	53	57	59		
Split left: primary row 2	5	2	61	63	67	69		
Opposites: twins left: & split right: alternate 1	6	3	71	73	77	79		1
Split right: primary row 1	7	1	81	83	87	89		
Single middle right: primary row 2	8	2	91	93	97	99		
Palindrome: seven associations row 3 only	9	3	101	103	107	109		&

47

Description	#		Col1	Col2	Col3	Col4	Extra
Single middle left: primary row 1.	10	1	111	113	117	119	
Single middle right: primary row 2	11	2	121	123	127	129	
Opposites: twins right: & split left: alternate 2	12	3	131	133	137	139	2
Single right: primary row 1	13	1	141	143	147	149	
Split left: primary row 2	14	2	151	153	157	159	
Twins removed	15	3	161	163	167	169	
Split right: primary row 1	16	1	171	173	177	179	
Single left: primary row 2	17	2	181	183	187	189	
Palindrome: seven associations row 3 only	18	3	191	193	197	199	&
Gray & white spaces	19	1	201	203	207	209	
Single left: primary row 2	20	2	211	213	217	219	
Twins removed: twins right: & split right: alternate 1	21	3	221	223	227	229	1
Split right: primary row 1	22	1	231	233	237	239	
Single left: primary row 2	23	2	241	243	247	249	
Split left: alternate 2	24	3	251	253	257	259	2
Split right: primary row 1	25	1	261	263	267	269	
Split left: primary row 2	26	2	271	273	277	279	
Twins left	27	3	281	283	287	289	
Single middle left: primary row 1	28	1	291	293	297	299	
Single middle right: primary row 2	29	2	301	303	307	309	
Twins removed; twins left: & Split left: alternate 2	30	3	311	313	317	319	2
Gray & white spaces	31	1	321	323	327	329	

Split left: primary row 2	32	2	331	333	337	339	
Twins right	33	3	341	343	347	349	
Split right: primary row 1	34	1	351	353	357	359	
Single middle right: primary row 2	35	2	361	363	_367_	369	
Split right: alternate 1	36	3	371	373	377	379	1
Split right: primary row 1	37	1	381	383	387	389	
Single middle right: primary row 2	38	2	391	393	_397_	399	
Opposites	39	3	401	403	407	409	
Single right: primary row 1	40	1	411	413	417	_419_	
Single left: primary row 2	41	2	_421_	423	427	429	
Opposites: twins left: & split right: alternate 1	42	3	431	433	437	439	1
Split right: primary row 1	43	1	441	443	447	449	
Single middle right: primary row 2	44	2	451	453	_457_	459	
Twins removed: twins left: & Split left: alternate 2	45	3	461	463	467	469	2
Single right: primary row 1	46	1	471	473	477	_479_	
Single middle right: primary row 2	47	2	481	483	_487_	489	
Opposites	48	3	491	493	497	499	
Split right: primary row 1	49	1	501	503	507	509	
White & gray spaces	50	2	511	513	517	519	
Twins left	51	3	521	523	527	529	
Gray & white spaces	52	1	531	533	537	539	
Split left: primary row 2	53	2	541	543	547	549	

Single middle right: alternate 2	54	3	551	553	_557_	559	2
Split right: primary row 1	55	1	561	563	567	569	
Split left: primary row 2	56	2	571	573	577	579	
Single middle right: alternate 2	57	3	581	583	_587_	589	2
Split right: primary row 1	58	1	591	593	597	599	
Split left: primary row 2	59	2	601	603	607	609	
Twins removed: twins right: & split right: alternate 1	60	3	611	613	617	619	1
Gray & white spaces	61	1	621	623	627	629	
Single left: primary row 2	62	2	_631_	633	637	639	
Twins removed: twins left: & Split left: alternate 2	63	3	641	643	647	649	2
Split right: primary row 1	64	1	651	653	657	659	
Single left: primary row 2	65	2	_661_	663	667	669	
Twins removed	66	3	671	673	677	679	
Single middle left: primary row 1	67	1	681	_683_	687	689	
Single left: primary row 2	68	2	_691_	693	697	699	
Opposites	69	3	701	703	707	709	
Single right: primary row 1	70	1	711	713	717	_719_	
Single middle right: primary row 2	71	2	721	723	_727_	729	
Split right: alternate 1	72	3	731	733	737	739	1
Single middle left: primary row 1	73	1	741	_743_	747	749	
Split left: primary row 2	74	2	751	753	757	759	
Opposites	75	3	761	763	767	769	

Description	#	Cycle					
Single middle left: primary row 1	76	1	771	*773*	777	779	
Single middle right: primary row 2	77	2	781	783	*787*	789	
Single middle right: alternate 2	78	3	791	793	*797*	799	2
Single right: primary row 1	79	1	801	803	807	*809*	
Single left: primary row 2	80	2	*811*	813	817	819	
Palindrome: seven associations row 3 only	81	3	821	823	827	829	&
Single right: primary row 1	82	1	831	833	837	*839*	
White & gray spaces	83	2	841	843	847	849	
Twins removed: twins right: & split right: alternate 1	84	3	851	853	857	859	1
Single middle left: primary row 1	85	1	861	*863*	867	869	
Single middle right: primary row 2	86	2	871	873	*877*	879	
Twins removed; twins left & Split left: alternate 2	87	3	881	883	887	889	2
Gray & white spaces	88	1	891	893	897	899	
Single middle right: primary row 2	89	2	901	903	*907*	909	
Opposites	90	3	911	913	917	919	
Single right: primary row 1	91	1	921	923	927	*929*	
Single middle right: primary row 2	92	2	931	933	*937*	939	
Split left: alternate 2	93	3	941	943	947	949	2
Single middle left: primary row 1.	94	1	951	*953*	957	959	
Single middle right: primary row 2	95	2	961	963	*967*	969	
Split left: alternate 2	96	3	971	973	977	979	2
Single middle left: primary row 1	97	1	981	*983*	987	989	

Description	#						
Split left: primary row 2	98	2	991	993	997	999	
Single right: alternate 1	99	3	1001	1003	1007	*1009*	1
Split right: primary row 1	100	1	1011	1013	1017	1019	
Single left: primary row 2	101	2	*1021*	1023	1027	1029	
Opposites, twins left & split right: alternate 1	102	3	1031	1033	1037	1039	1
Single left: primary row 1	103	1	1041	1043	1047	*1049*	
Single left: primary row 2	104	2	*1051*	1053	1057	1059	
Opposites: twins left: & split right: alternate 1	105	3	1061	1063	1067	1069	1
Gray & white spaces	106	1	1071	1073	1077	1079	
Single middle right: primary row 2	107	2	1081	1083	*1087*	1089	
Twins removed; twins left & Split left: alternate 2	108	3	1091	1093	1097	1099	2
Split right: primary row 1	109	1	1101	1103	1107	1109	
Single middle right: primary row 2	110	2	1111	1113	*1117*	1119	
Split right: alternate 1	111	3	1121	1123	1127	1129	1
Gray & white spaces	112	1	1131	1133	1137	1139	
White & gray spaces	113	2	1141	1143	1147	1149	
Twins left	114	3	1151	1153	1157	1159	
Single middle left: primary row 1	115	1	1161	*1163*	1167	1169	
Single left: primary row 2	116	2	*1171*	1173	1177	1179	
Split left: alternate 2	117	3	1181	1183	1187	1189	2
Single middle left: primary row 1	118	1	1191	*1193*	1197	1199	
Single left: primary row 2	119	2	*1201*	1203	1207	1209	

Twins removed	120	3	1211	1213	1217	1219	
Split right: primary row 1	121	1	1221	1223	1227	1229	
Split left: primary row 2	122	2	1231	1233	1237	1239	
Single right: alternate 1	123	3	1241	1243	1247	1249	1
Single right: primary row 1	124	1	1251	1253	1257	1259	
White & gray spaces	125	2	1261	1263	1267	1269	
Twins right	126	3	1271	1273	1277	1279	
Split right: primary row 1	127	1	1281	1283	1287	1289	
Split left: primary row 2	128	2	1291	1293	1297	1299	
Twins removed; twins left & Split left: alternate 2	129	3	1301	1303	1307	1309	2
Single left: primary row 1	130	1	1311	1313	1317	1319	
Split left: primary row 2	131	2	1321	1323	1327	1329	
White spaces	132	3	1331	1333	1337	1339	
Gray & white spaces	133	1	1341	1343	1347	1349	
White & gray spaces	134	2	1351	1353	1357	1359	
Split left: alternate 2	135	3	1361	1363	1367	1369	2
Single middle left: primary row 1	136	1	1371	1373	1377	1379	
Single left: primary row 2	137	2	1381	1383	1387	1389	
Single right: alternate 1	138	3	1391	1393	1397	1399	1
Single right: primary row 1	139	1	1401	1403	1407	1409	
White & gray spaces	140	2	1411	1413	1417	1419	
Twins removed: twins right: & split right: alternate 1	141	3	1421	1423	1427	1429	1
Split right: primary row 1	142	1	1431	1433	1437	1439	

53

Description	#						
Single middle right: primary row 2	143	2	1441	1443	*1447*	1449	
Opposites: twins left: & split right: alternate 1	144	3	**1451**	1453	1457	**1459**	1
Gray and white spaces	145	1	1461	1463	1467	1469	
Single left: primary row 2	146	2	*1471*	1473	1477	1479	
Palindrome: seven associations row 3 only	147	3	**1481**	**1483**	**1487**	**1489**	&
Split right: primary row 1	148	1	1491	1493	1497	1499	
White & gray spaces	149	2	1501	1503	1507	1509	
Single left: alternate 2	150	3	*1511*	1513	1517	1519	2
Single middle left: primary row 1	151	1	1521	*1523*	1527	1529	
Single left: primary row 2	152	2	*1531*	1533	1537	1539	
Split right: alternate 1	153	3	1541	1543	1547	1549	1
Split right: primary row 1	154	1	1551	1553	1557	1559	
Single middle right: primary row 2	155	2	1561	1563	*1567*	1569	
Opposites	156	3	**1571**	1573	1577	**1579**	
Single middle left: primary row 1	157	1	1581	*1583*	1587	1589	
Single middle right: primary row 2	158	2	1591	1593	*1597*	1599	
Opposites: twins right: & split left: alternate 2	159	3	**1601**	1603	1607	**1609**	2
Split right: primary row 1	160	1	1611	1613	1617	1619	
Split left: primary row 2	161	2	1621	1623	1627	1629	
Single middle right: alternate XXXX	162	3	1631	1633	*1637*	1639	2
Gray & white spaces	163	1	1641	1643	1647	1649	
Single middle right: primary row 2	164	2	1651	1653	*1657*	1659	

Description	#						
Twins removed: twins right: & split right: alternate 1	165	3	1661	1663	1667	1669	1
Gray & white spaces	166	1	1671	1673	1677	1679	
White & gray spaces	167	2	1681	1683	1687	1689	
Twins removed: twins right: & split right: alternate 1	168	3	1691	1693	1697	1699	1
Single right: primary row 1	169	1	1701	1703	1707	1709	
White & gray spaces	170	2	1711	1713	1717	1719	
Twins left	171	3	1721	1723	1727	1729	
Single middle left: primary row 1	172	1	1731	1733	1737	1739	
Split left: primary row 2	173	2	1741	1743	1747	1749	
Split right: alternate 1	174	3	1751	1753	1757	1759	1
Gray & white spaces	175	1	1761	1763	1767	1769	
Single middle right: primary row 2	176	2	1771	1773	1777	1779	
Twins removed: twins right: & split right: alternate 1	177	3	1781	1783	1787	1789	1
Gray & white spaces	178	1	1791	1793	1797	1799	
Single left: primary row 2	179	2	1801	1803	1807	1809	
Single left: alternate 2	180	3	1811	1813	1817	1819	2
Single middle left: primary row 1	181	1	1821	1823	1827	1829	
Single left: primary row 2	182	2	1831	1833	1837	1839	
Single middle right: alternate 2	183	3	1841	1843	1847	1849	2
Gray & white spaces	184	1	1851	1853	1857	1859	
Split left: primary row 2	185	2	1861	1863	1867	1869	
Palindrome: seven associations row 3 only	186	3	1871	1873	1877	1879	&

Single right: primary row 1	187	1	1881	1883	1887	1889	
White & gray spaces	188	2	1891	1893	1897	1899	
Split left: alternate 2	189	3	1901	1903	1907	1909	2
Single middle left: primary row 1	190	1	1911	1913	1917	1919	
White & gray spaces	191	2	1921	1923	1927	1929	
Twins left	192	3	1931	1933	1937	1939	
Single right: primary row 1	193	1	1941	1943	1947	1949	
Single left: primary row 2	194	2	1951	1953	1957	1959	
White spaces	195	3	1961	1963	1967	1969	
Split right: primary row 1	196	1	1971	1973	1977	1979	
Single middle right: primary row 2	197	2	1981	1983	1987	1989	
Twins removed: twins right: & split right: alternate 1	198	3	1991	1993	1997	1999	1
Single middle left: primary row 1	199	1	2001	2003	2007	2009	
Split left: primary row 2	200	2	2011	2013	2017	2019	
Twins right	201	3	2021	2023	2027	2029	

Table 4. Prime number proof (digits 1–2,000)

Appendix B

Associations and Weights of Prime Numbers

(See chapter 5 for details of weights and percentages per 10,000 rows, for 10 sections.)
Original Proof Was To 100,000 Shown in Weight Tables Chapter 5.
Table Below Is To 2,000,
However, Totals Are To 100,000 Digits

(Table 5)

Single digits of 1, 2, 3, 5, & 7 (super palindrome) not weighted, or tallied in the percentages

LINE	ROW	PALINDROME		TWINS REMOVED		OPPOSITES		TWINS LEFT		TWINS RIGHT		SPLIT LEFT ROW 2 (3)		SPLIT RIGHT ROW 1 (3)	
		\<-- ROW 3 PRIMARY ONLY --\>													
		AL	PR	AL	PR	AL	PR	AL	PR	AL	PR	AL (3)	PR 2	AL (3)	PR 1
TOTAL (WEIGHT)		0	37	0	422	0	405	0	401	0	407	421	823	383	796
00	X	Totals for alternates (AL) and primaries (PR) are for 10,000 rows Columns 1, 3, 7 & 9													
0	3	1		1		1		1		1		1	1	1	1
1	1		(only row 3)									(all rows)			1
2	2												1		
3	3			1				1				1	1		
4	1														1
5	2												1		
6	3					1		1						1	1
7	1														1
8	2														

		1	2	3	4	5	6	7	8	9	10	11	12	13
9	3	1		1		1		1		1	1	1	1	1
10	1													
11	2													
12	3					1				1	1	1		
13	1													
14	2											1		
15	3			1										
16	1													1
17	2													
18	3	1		1		1		1		1	1	1	1	1
19	1													
20	2													
21	3			1						1			1	1
22	1													1
23	2													
24	3										1	1		
25	1													1
26	2											1		
27	3							1						
28	1													
29	2													
30	3			1				1			1	1		
31	1													
32	2											1		
33	3									1				
34	1													1
35	2													
36	3												1	1
37	1													1
38	2													
39	3					1								
40	1													
41	2													
42	3					1		1					1	1
43	1													1
44	2													
45	3			1				1			1	1		

Row											
46	1										
47	2										
48	3	■	■	1	■	■					
49	1										1
50	2										
51	3	■	■	■	1	■					
52	1										
53	2								1		
54	3	■	■	■	■	■					
55	1										1
56	2								1		
57	3	■	■	■	■	■					
58	1										1
59	2								1		
60	3	■	1	■	■	1				1	1
61	1										
62	2										
63	3	■	1	■	1	■	1	1			
64	1										1
65	2										
66	3	■	1	■	■	■					
67	1										
68	2										
69	3	■	■	1	■	■					
70	1										
71	2										
72	3	■	■	■	■	■				1	1
73	1										
74	2								1		
75	3	■	■	1	■	■					
76	1										
77	2										
78	3	■	■	■	■	■					
79	1										
80	2										
81	3	1	1	1	1	1	1	1	1	1	
82	1										

83	2										
84	3	■	**1**	■	■	**1**			**1**	**1**	
85	1										
86	2										
87	3	■	**1**	■	■	■	**1**	**1**			
88	1										
89	2										
90	3	■	■	**1**	■	■					
91	1										
92	2										
93	3	■	■	■	■	■	**1**	**1**			
94	1										
95	2										
96	3	■	■	■	■	■	**1**	**1**			
97	1										
98	2								**1**		
99	3	■	■	■	■	■					
100	1									**1**	
101	2										
102	3	■	■	**1**	**1**	■			**1**	**1**	
103	1										
104	2										
105	3	■	■	**1**	**1**	■			**1**	**1**	
106	1										
107	2										
108	3	■	**1**	■	**1**	■	**1**	**1**			
109	1									**1**	
110	2										
111	3	■	■	■	■	■			**1**	**1**	
112	1										
113	2										
114	3	■	■	■	**1**	■					
115	1										
116	2										
117	3	■	■	■	■	■	**1**	**1**			
118	1										
119	2										

120	3
121	1
122	2
123	3
124	1
125	2
126	3
127	1
128	2
129	3
130	1
131	2
132	3
133	1
134	2
135	3
136	1
137	2
138	3
139	1
140	2
141	3
142	1
143	2
144	3
145	1
146	2
147	3
148	1
149	2
150	3
151	1
152	2
153	3
154	1
155	2
156	3

Row	#	1	2	3	4	5	6	7	8	9	10
157	1							▓		▓	
158	2							▓		▓	
159	3	■	■	1	■	1	1	1	▓	▓	
160	1							▓			1
161	2							1			
162	3	■	■	■	■	■	▓	▓	▓	▓	▓
163	1							▓			
164	2							▓			
165	3	■	1	■	■	1	▓		1	1	
166	1							▓			
167	2							▓			
168	3	■	1	■	■	1	▓		1	1	
169	1							▓			
170	2							▓			
171	3	■	■	■	1	■	▓	▓			
172	1							▓			
173	2							1			
174	3	■	■	■	■	■	▓		1	1	
175	1							▓			
176	2							▓			
177	3	■	1	■	■	1	▓		1	1	
178	1							▓			
179	2							▓			
180	3	■	■	■	■	■	▓	▓	▓	▓	▓
181	1							▓			
182	2							▓			
183	3	■	■	■	■	■	▓	▓	▓	▓	▓
184	1							▓			
185	2							1			
186	3	1	1	1	1	1	1	1	1	1	
187	1							▓			
188	2							▓			
189	3	■	■	■	■	■	1	1	▓	▓	
190	1							▓			
191	2							▓			
192	3	■	■	■	1	■	▓	▓	▓	▓	
193	1							▓		▓	

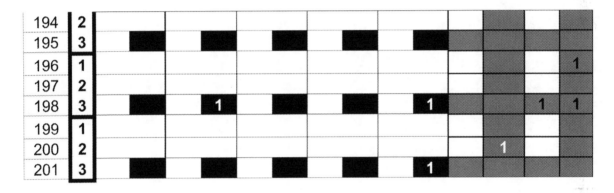

Table 5. Pair prime, singles, and associations—weights and percentages

Appendix C

Red Singles Calculated

(See chapter 6 for details about red singles)
Original Proof Was To 100,000 Shown in Weight Tables Chapter 6.
Table Below Is To 2,000,
However, Totals Are To 100,000 Digits

(Table 6)

LINES	ROWS	RED PRIME WEIGHTS (1 EACH/WEIGHT)								ALT. & PRI. WEIGHTS
		1	1	3	3	7	7	9	9	COLUMNS
		Alt.	Pri.	Alt.	Pri.	Alt.	Pri.	Alt.	Pri.	ALTERNATES/PRIMARY
		(323)	1107	(329)	1129	(302)	1099	(322)	1120	TOTALS PER COLUMN
00	X									FIRST 100,000 DIGITS
0	3									
1	1									
2	2									
3	3	☐		☐		☐		☐		
4	1									
5	2									
6	3	☐		☐		☐		☐		
7	1									
8	2						1			SINGLE PRIMARY 0/1
9	3	☐		☐		☐		☐		
10	1				1					SINGLE PRIMARY 0/1
11	2						1			SINGLE PRIMARY 0/1
12	3	☐		☐		☐		☐		
13	1								1	SINGLE PRIMARY 0/1
14	2									
15	3	☐		☐		☐		☐		

#		Col 1	Col 2	Col 3	Col 4	
16	1					
17	2	1				**SINGLE PRIMARY 0/1**
18	3	☐	☐	☐	☐	
19	1					
20	2	1				**SINGLE PRIMARY 0/1**
21	3	☐	☐	☐	☐	
22	1					
23	2	1				**SINGLE PRIMARY 0/1**
24	3	☐	☐	☐	☐	
25	1					
26	2					
27	3		☐	☐	☐	
28	1		1			**SINGLE PRIMARY 0/1**
29	2			1		**SINGLE PRIMARY 0/1**
30	3	☐	☐	☐	☐	
31	1					
32	2					
33	3	☐	☐	☐	☐	
34	1					
35	2			1		**SINGLE PRIMARY 0/1**
36	3	☐	☐	☐	☐	
37	1					
38	2			1		**SINGLE PRIMARY 0/1**
39	3	☐	☐	☐	☐	
40	1				1	**SINGLE PRIMARY 0/1**
41	2	1				**SINGLE PRIMARY 0/1**
42	3	☐	☐	☐	☐	
43	1					
44	2			1		**SINGLE PRIMARY 0/1**
45	3	☐	☐	☐	☐	
46	1				1	**SINGLE PRIMARY 0/1**
47	2			1		**SINGLE PRIMARY 0/1**
48	3	☐	☐	☐	☐	
49	1					
50	2					
51	3	☐	☐	☐	☐	

No.	Pos							Label
52	1							
53	2							
54	3	☐		☐	1	1	☐	ALTERNATE (WEIGHT 1/1)
55	1							
56	2							
57	3	☐		☐	1	1	☐	ALTERNATE (WEIGHT 1/1)
58	1							
59	2							
60	3	☐		☐		☐	☐	
61	1							
62	2		1					SINGLE PRIMARY 0/1
63	3	☐		☐		☐	☐	
64	1							
65	2		1					SINGLE PRIMARY 0/1
66	3	☐		☐		☐	☐	
67	1			1				SINGLE PRIMARY 0/1
68	2		1					SINGLE PRIMARY 0/1
69	3	☐		☐		☐	☐	
70	1						1	SINGLE PRIMARY 0/1
71	2					1		SINGLE PRIMARY 0/1
72	3	☐		☐		☐	☐	
73	1			1				SINGLE PRIMARY 0/1
74	2							
75	3	☐		☐		☐	☐	
76	1			1				SINGLE PRIMARY 0/1
77	2					1		SINGLE PRIMARY 0/1
78	3	☐		☐	1	1	☐	ALTERNATE (WEIGHT 1/1)
79	1						1	SINGLE PRIMARY 0/1
80	2		1					SINGLE PRIMARY 0/1
81	3	☐		☐		☐	☐	
82	1						1	SINGLE PRIMARY 0/1
83	2							
84	3	☐		☐		☐	☐	
85	1			1				SINGLE PRIMARY 0/1
86	2					1		SINGLE PRIMARY 0/1
87	3	☐		☐		☐	☐	

#	Pos	Col1	Col2	Col3	Col4	Col5	Note
88	1						
89	2			1			SINGLE PRIMARY 0/1
90	3	□					
91	1					1	SINGLE PRIMARY 0/1
92	2			1			SINGLE PRIMARY 0/1
93	3	□					
94	1		1				SINGLE PRIMARY 0/1
95	2			1			SINGLE PRIMARY 0/1
96	3	□					
97	1		1				SINGLE PRIMARY 0/1
98	2						
99	3	□			1	1	ALTERNATE (WEIGHT 1/1)
100	1						
101	2	1					SINGLE PRIMARY 0/1
102	3	□					
103	1					1	SINGLE PRIMARY 0/1
104	2	1					SINGLE PRIMARY 0/1
105	3	□					
106	1						
107	2			1			SINGLE PRIMARY 0/1
108	3	□					
109	1						
110	2			1			SINGLE PRIMARY 0/1
111	3	□					
112	1						
113	2						
114	3	□					
115	1		1				SINGLE PRIMARY 0/1
116	2	1					SINGLE PRIMARY 0/1
117	3	□					
118	1		1				SINGLE PRIMARY 0/1
119	2	1					SINGLE PRIMARY 0/1
120	3	□					
121	1						
122	2						
123	3	□			1	1	ALTERNATE (WEIGHT 1/1)

Row		Note
124	1	1 — SINGLE PRIMARY 0/1
125	2	
126	3	
127	1	
128	2	
129	3	
130	1	1 — SINGLE PRIMARY 0/1
131	2	
132	3	
133	1	
134	2	
135	3	
136	1	1 — SINGLE PRIMARY 0/1
137	2	1 — SINGLE PRIMARY 0/1
138	3	1 1 — ALTERNATE (WEIGHT 1/1)
139	1	1 — SINGLE PRIMARY 0/1
140	2	
141	3	
142	1	
143	2	1 — SINGLE PRIMARY
144	3	
145	1	
146	2	1 — SINGLE PRIMARY 0/1
147	3	
148	1	
149	2	
150	3	1 1 — ALTERNATE (WEIGHT 1/1)
151	1	1 — SINGLE PRIMARY
152	2	1 — SINGLE PRIMARY
153	3	
154	1	
155	2	1 — SINGLE PRIMARY
156	3	
157	1	1 — SINGLE PRIMARY 0/1
158	2	1 — SINGLE PRIMARY 0/1
159	3	

#							
160	1						
161	2						
162	3	☐	☐	1	1	☐	ALTERNATE (WEIGHT 1/1)
163	1						
164	2			1			SINGLE PRIMARY 0/1
165	3	☐	☐	☐	☐		
166	1						
167	2						
168	3	☐	☐	☐	☐		
169	1					1	SINGLE PRIMARY
170	2						
171	3	☐	☐	☐	☐		
172	1		1				SINGLE PRIMARY
173	2						
174	3	☐	☐	☐	☐		
175	1						
176	2			1			SINGLE PRIMARY 0/1
177	3	☐	☐	☐	☐		
178	1						
179	2	1					SINGLE PRIMARY 0/1
180	3	1	1	☐	☐	☐	ALTERNATE (WEIGHT 1/1)
181	1		1				SINGLE PRIMARY 0/1
182	2	1					SINGLE PRIMARY 0/1
183	3	☐	☐	1	1	☐	ALTERNATE (WEIGHT 1/1)
184	1						
185	2						
186	3	☐	☐	☐	☐		
187	1					1	SINGLE PRIMARY 0/1
188	2						
189	3	☐	☐	☐			
190	1		1				SINGLE PRIMARY 0/1
191	2						
192	3	☐	☐	☐	☐		
193	1					1	SINGLE PRIMARY 0/1
194	2	1					

195	3	☐	☐	☐	☐		
196	1						
197	2				1		SINGLE PRIMARY 0/1
198	3	☐	☐	☐	☐		
199	1			1			SINGLE PRIMARY 0/1
200	2						
201	3	☐	☐	☐	☐		

Table 6. Red singles weights counted

Appendix D

Unit Prime Gray Spaces Calculation Matrix

(Duplicated - Same as <u>Chapter 7</u>, Table Series 2A through 2D)
UNIT MATRIX PRIME GRAY SPACES CALCULATION
MATRIX - TYPICAL FOR ALL ROWS 1 - 2

UNIT MATRIX PRIME GRAY SPACES CALCULATION MATRIX - TYPICAL FOR ALL ROWS 1 - 2 - 3

EXAMPLE $\dfrac{21}{3} = 7.000$ If a prime ending in "ONE" is divided by unit prime 3 it will produce a decimal of the following:	SEE "UNIT MATRIX PRIME WHITE SPACE MATRIX" COLUMN 1, FOR WHITE SPACES STARTING AT PRIME UNIT 7 THE SEQUENCE IS THE UNIT MATRIX PRIME NUMERATOR	LINES	ROWS	COLUMN 1	UNIT Calculations 3
Row 1 will produce a decimal of n.000 (ZEE Gray Space). Whole number is a space.		1	1	⊠ 21	7.000
Row 2 will produce a decimal of n.333. Decimal is not a space - possible prime.		2	2	31	10.33333333
Row 3 will produce a decimal of n.667. Decimal is not a space - possible prime.		3	3	41	13.66666667

Table 2Ad. Unit matrix prime gray column 1

UNIT MATRIX PRIME GRAY SPACES CALCULATION MATRIX - TYPICAL FOR ALL ROWS 1 - 2 - 3

EXAMPLE $\dfrac{33}{3} = 11.000$ If a prime ending in "THREE" is divided by unit prime 3 it will produce a decimal of the following:	SEE "UNIT MATRIX PRIME WHITE SPACE MATRIX" COLUMN 3, FOR WHITE SPACES STARTING AT PRIME UNIT 7 THE SEQUENCE IS THE UNIT MATRIX PRIME NUMERATOR	LINES	ROWS	COLUMN 3	3
Row 1 will produce a decimal of n.667. Decimal is not a space - possible prime.		1	1	23	7.66666667
Row 2 will produce a decimal of n.000. (ZEE Gray Space). Whole number is a space.		2	2	⊠ 33	11.000
Row 3 will produce a decimal of n.333. Decimal is not a space - possible prime		3	3	43	14.33333333

Table 2Bd. Unit matrix prime gray column 3

EXAMPLE $\dfrac{27}{3} = 9.000$ If a prime ending in "SEVEN" is divided by unit prime 3 it will produce a decimal of the following:	SEE "UNIT MATRIX PRIME WHITE SPACE MATRIX" COLUMN 7, FOR WHITE SPACES STARTING AT PRIME UNIT 7 THE SEQUENCE IS THE UNIT MATRIX PRIME NUMERATOR	L I N E S	R O W S	C O L U M N 7	UNIT Calculations 3
Row 1 will produce a decimal of n.000 (ZEE Gray Space). Whole number is a space.		1	1	27	9.000
Row 2 will produce a decimal of n.333. Decimal is not a space - possible prime.		2	2	37	12.33333333
Row 3 will produce a decimal of n.667. Decimal is not a space - possible prime.		3	3	47	15.66666667

Table 2Cd. Unit matrix prime gray column 7

EXAMPLE $\dfrac{39}{3} = 13.000$ If a prime ending in "NINE" is divided by unit prime 3 it will produce a decimal of the following:	SEE "UNIT MATRIX PRIME WHITE SPACE MATRIX" COLUMN 9, FOR WHITE SPACES STARTING AT PRIME UNIT 7 THE SEQUENCE IS THE UNIT MATRIX PRIME NUMERATOR	L I N E S	R O W S	C O L U M N 9	UNIT Calculations 3
Row 1 will produce a decimal of n.667. Decimal is not a space - possible prime.		1	1	29	9.66666667
Row 2 will produce a decimal of n.000. (ZEE Gray Space). Whole number is a space.		2	2	39	13.000
Row 3 will produce a decimal of n.333. Decimal is not a space - possible prime		3	3	49	16.33333333

Table 2Dd. Unit matrix prime gray column 9

LINE	ROW	COLUMN 1	COLUMN 2	COLUMN 3	COLUMN 4	ALTERNATE
1	1	21	23	27	29	
2	2	31	33	37	39	
3	3	41	43	47	49	
4	1	51	53	57	59	
5	2	61	63	67	69	
6	3	71	73	77	79	

Figure 16d. Typical gray space configuration "Zees" same as *chapter 7*

Appendix E

White Spaces Calculated

(See chapter 8 for white space explanations and how to calculate white open spaces.)
Original Proof Was To 100,000 Shown in Weight Tables Chapter 8.
Table Below Is To 2,000,
However, Totals Are To 100,000 Digits
Calculation totals are per column of 10,000

(Table 7)

LINES	ROWS	WHITE OPEN – WEIGHT BY COLUMN (Non-prime)				FOR TOTAL SPACES ADD 4/12 LINES FOR GRAY
		1	3	7	9	
		(NO GRAYS COUNTED)				
		4280	4266	4255	4273	TOTALS
00	X					Per Column 100,000
0	3					
1	1					Typical Grays Not Shown
2	2					
3	3				1	White Space (Wt. 1)
4	1					
5	2					
6	3			1		White Space (Wt. 1)
7	1					
8	2	1				White Space (Wt. 1)
9	3					
10	1				1	White Space (Wt. 1)
11	2	1				White Space (Wt. 1)
12	3		1			White Space (Wt. 1)
13	1		1			White Space (Wt. 1)

14	2					
15	3	1			1	White Space (Wt. 1)
16	1					
17	2			1		White Space (Wt. 1)
18	3					
19	1		1		1	White Space (Wt. 1)
20	2			1		White Space (Wt. 1)
21	3	1				White Space (Wt. 1)
22	1					
23	2			1		White Space (Wt. 1)
24	3		1		1	White Space (Wt. 1)
25	1					
26	2					
27	3			1	1	White Space (Wt. 1)
28	1				1	White Space (Wt. 1)
29	2	1				White Space (Wt. 1)
30	3				1	White Space (Wt. 1)
31	1		1		1	White Space (Wt. 1)
32	2					
33	3	1	1			White Space (Wt. 1)
34	1					
35	2	1				White Space (Wt. 1)
36	3	1		1		White Space (Wt. 1)
37	1					
38	2	1				White Space (Wt. 1)
39	3		1	1		White Space (Wt. 1)
40	1		1			White Space (Wt. 1)
41	2			1		White Space (Wt. 1)
42	3			1		White Space (Wt. 1)
43	1					
44	2	1				White Space (Wt. 1)

76

45	3				1	White Space (Wt. 1)
46	1		1			White Space (Wt. 1)
47	2	1				White Space (Wt. 1)
48	3		1	1		White Space (Wt. 1)
49	1					
50	2	1		1		White Space (Wt. 1)
51	3			1	1	White Space (Wt. 1)
52	1		1		1	White Space (Wt. 1)
53	2					
54	3	1	1		1	White Space (Wt. 1)
55	1					
56	2					
57	3	1	1		1	White Space (Wt. 1)
58	1					
59	2					
60	3	1				White Space (Wt. 1)
61	1		1		1	White Space (Wt. 1)
62	2			1		White Space (Wt. 1)
63	3				1	White Space (Wt. 1)
64	1					
65	2			1		White Space (Wt. 1)
66	3	1			1	White Space (Wt. 1)
67	1				1	White Space (Wt. 1)
68	2			1		White Space (Wt. 1)
69	3		1	1		White Space (Wt. 1)
70	1		1			White Space (Wt. 1)
71	2	1				White Space (Wt. 1)
72	3	1		1		White Space (Wt. 1)
73	1				1	White Space (Wt. 1)
74	2					
75	3		1	1		White Space (Wt. 1)

#		A	B	C	D	Notes
76	1				1	White Space (Wt. 1)
77	2	1				White Space (Wt. 1)
78	3	1	1		1	White Space (Wt. 1)
79	1		1			White Space (Wt. 1)
80	2			1		White Space (Wt. 1)
81	3					
82	1		1			White Space (Wt. 1)
83	2	1		1		White Space (Wt. 1)
84	3	1				White Space (Wt. 1)
85	1				1	White Space (Wt. 1)
86	2	1				White Space (Wt. 1)
87	3				1	White Space (Wt. 1)
88	1		1		1	White Space (Wt. 1)
89	2	1				White Space (Wt. 1)
90	3		1	1		White Space (Wt. 1)
91	1		1			White Space (Wt. 1)
92	2	1				White Space (Wt. 1)
93	3		1		1	White Space (Wt. 1)
94	1				1	White Space (Wt. 1)
95	2	1				White Space (Wt. 1)
96	3		1		1	White Space (Wt. 1)
97	1				1	White Space (Wt. 1)
98	2					
99	3	1	1	1		White Space (Wt. 1)
100	1					
101	2			1		White Space (Wt. 1)
102	3			1		White Space (Wt. 1)
103	1		1			White Space (Wt. 1)
104	2			1		White Space (Wt. 1)
105	3			1		White Space (Wt. 1)
106	1		1		1	White Space (Wt. 1)

107	2	1				White Space (Wt. 1)
108	3				1	White Space (Wt. 1)
109	1					
110	2	1				White Space (Wt. 1)
111	3	1		1		White Space (Wt. 1)
112	1		1		1	White Space (Wt. 1)
113	2	1		1		White Space (Wt. 1)
114	3			1	1	White Space (Wt. 1)
115	1				1	White Space (Wt. 1)
116	2			1		White Space (Wt. 1)
117	3		1		1	White Space (Wt. 1)
118	1				1	White Space (Wt. 1)
119	2			1		White Space (Wt. 1)
120	3	1			1	White Space (Wt. 1)
121	1					
122	2					
123	3	1	1	1		White Space (Wt. 1)
124	1		1			White Space (Wt. 1)
125	2	1		1		White Space (Wt. 1)
126	3	1	1			White Space (Wt. 1)
127	1					
128	2					
129	3				1	White Space (Wt. 1)
130	1		1			White Space (Wt. 1)
131	2					
132	3	1	1	1	1	White Space (Wt. 1)
133	1		1		1	White Space (Wt. 1)
134	2	1		1		White Space (Wt. 1)
135	3		1		1	White Space (Wt. 1)
136	1				1	White Space (Wt. 1)
137	2			1		White Space (Wt. 1)

138	3	1	1	1		White Space (Wt. 1)
139	1		1			White Space (Wt. 1)
140	2	1		1		White Space (Wt. 1)
141	3	1				White Space (Wt. 1)
142	1					
143	2	1				White Space (Wt. 1)
144	3			1		White Space (Wt. 1)
145	1		1		1	White Space (Wt. 1)
146	2			1		White Space (Wt. 1)
147	3					
148	1					
149	2	1		1		White Space (Wt. 1)
150	3		1	1	1	White Space (Wt. 1)
151	1				1	White Space (Wt. 1)
152	2			1		White Space (Wt. 1)
153	3	1		1		White Space (Wt. 1)
154	1					
155	2	1				White Space (Wt. 1)
156	3		1	1		White Space (Wt. 1)
157	1				1	White Space (Wt. 1)
158	2	1				White Space (Wt. 1)
159	3		1			White Space (Wt. 1)
160	1					
161	2					
162	3	1	1		1	White Space (Wt. 1)
163	1		1		1	White Space (Wt. 1)
164	2	1				White Space (Wt. 1)
165	3	1				White Space (Wt. 1)
166	1		1		1	White Space (Wt. 1)
167	2	1		1		White Space (Wt. 1)
168	3	1				White Space (Wt. 1)
169	1		1			White Space (Wt. 1)

170	2	1		1		White Space (Wt. 1)
171	3			1	1	White Space (Wt. 1)
172	1				1	White Space (Wt. 1)
173	2					
174	3	1		1		White Space (Wt. 1)
175	1		1		1	White Space (Wt. 1)
176	2	1				White Space (Wt. 1)
177	3	1				White Space (Wt. 1)
178	1		1		1	White Space (Wt. 1)
179	2			1		White Space (Wt. 1)
180	3		1	1	1	White Space (Wt. 1)
181	1				1	White Space (Wt. 1)
182	2			1		White Space (Wt. 1)
183	3	1	1		1	White Space (Wt. 1)
184	1		1		1	White Space (Wt. 1)
185	2					
186	3					
187	1		1			White Space (Wt. 1)
188	2	1		1		White Space (Wt. 1)
189	3		1		1	White Space (Wt. 1)
190	1				1	White Space (Wt. 1)
191	2	1		1		White Space (Wt. 1)
192	3			1	1	White Space (Wt. 1)
193	1		1			White Space (Wt. 1)
194	2			1		White Space (Wt. 1)
195	3	1	1	1	1	White Space (Wt. 1)
196	1					
197	2	1				White Space (Wt. 1)
198	3	1				White Space (Wt. 1)
199	1				1	White Space (Wt. 1)
200	2					
201	3	1	1			White Space (Wt. 1)

Table 7. White spaces of unit primes

81

Appendix F

Unit Prime White Space Matrix Column 1

(See chapter 8 for white space explanations and how to calculate white open spaces)

(Table 7A)

LINES	ROWS	COLUMN 1	UNIT PRIME WHITE SPACE MATRIX: COLUMN 1 WHOLE NUMBERS OTHER THAN ONE ARE SPACES EXAMPLE: *TABLE CELL* **91** ÷ BY *UNIT CELL* **7** = **13**				
			UNIT 2 COL 1 NO SPACES	UNIT 3 COL 1 GRAY SPACES	UNIT 5 COL 1 NO SPACES	UNIT 7 COL 1 WHITE SPACES	UNIT 11 COL 1 WHITE SPACES
			NO WHITE SPACES 2	REPEATS DOWN EVERY 3	NO WHITE SPACES 5	REPEATS DOWN EVERY 7	REPEATS DOWN EVERY 11
0	3	11	5.5	3.666	2.2	1.571	1
1	1	21	10.5	7	4.2	3	1.909
2	2	31	15.5	10.333	6.2	4.428	2.818
3	3	41	20.5	13.666	8.2	5.857	3.727
4	1	51	25.5	17	10.2	7.285	4.636
5	2	61	30.5	20.333	12.2	8.714	5.545
6	3	71	35.5	23.666	14.2	10.142	6.454
7	1	81	40.5	27	16.2	11.571	7.363
8	2	91	45.5	30.333	18.2	13	8.272
9	3	101	50.5	33.666	20.2	14.428	9.181
10	1	111	55.5	37	22.2	15.857	10.09
11	2	121	60.5	40.333	24.2	17.285	11
12	3	131	65.5	43.666	26.2	18.714	11.909
13	1	141	70.5	47	28.2	20.142	12.818

14	2	151	75.5	50.333	30.2	21.571	13.727
15	3	161	80.5	53.666	32.2	23	14.636
16	1	~~171~~	85.5	~~57~~	34.2	24.428	15.545
17	2	*181*	90.5	60.333	36.2	25.857	16.454
18	3	191	95.5	63.666	38.2	27.285	17.363
19	1	~~201~~	100.5	~~67~~	40.2	28.714	18.272
20	2	*211*	105.5	70.333	42.2	30.142	19.181
21	3	221	110.5	73.666	44.2	31.571	20.09
22	1	~~231~~	115.5	~~77~~	46.2	33	21
23	2	*241*	120.5	80.333	48.2	34.428	21.909
24	3	251	125.5	83.666	50.2	35.857	22.818
25	1	~~261~~	130.5	~~87~~	52.2	37.285	23.727
26	2	271	135.5	90.333	54.2	38.714	24.636
27	3	281	140.5	93.666	56.2	40.142	25.545
28	1	~~291~~	145.5	~~97~~	58.2	41.571	26.454
29	2	301	150.5	100.333	60.2	43	27.363
30	3	311	155.5	103.666	62.2	44.428	28.272
31	1	~~321~~	160.5	~~107~~	64.2	45.857	29.181
32	2	331	165.5	110.333	66.2	47.285	30.09
33	3	341	170.5	113.666	68.2	48.714	31
34	1	~~351~~	175.5	~~117~~	70.2	50.142	31.909
35	2	361	180.5	120.333	72.2	51.571	32.818
36	3	371	185.5	123.666	74.2	53	33.727
37	1	~~381~~	190.5	~~127~~	76.2	54.428	34.636
38	2	391	195.5	130.333	78.2	55.857	35.545
39	3	401	200.5	133.666	80.2	57.285	36.454
40	1	~~411~~	205.5	~~137~~	82.2	58.714	37.363
41	2	*421*	210.5	140.333	84.2	60.142	38.272
42	3	431	215.5	143.666	86.2	61.571	39.181
43	1	~~441~~	220.5	~~147~~	88.2	63	40.09

84

44	2	**451**	225.5	150.333	90.2	64.428	41
45	3	461	230.5	153.666	92.2	65.857	41.909
46	1	~~471~~	235.5	~~157~~	94.2	67.285	42.818
47	2	**481**	240.5	160.333	96.2	68.714	43.727
48	3	**491**	245.5	163.666	98.2	70.142	44.636
49	1	~~501~~	250.5	~~167~~	100.2	71.571	45.545
50	2	**511**	255.5	170.333	102.2	73	46.454
51	3	**521**	260.5	173.666	104.2	74.428	47.363
52	1	~~531~~	265.5	~~177~~	106.2	75.857	48.272
53	2	**541**	270.5	180.333	108.2	77.285	49.181
54	3	**551**	275.5	183.666	110.2	78.714	50.09
55	1	~~561~~	280.5	~~187~~	112.2	80.142	51
56	2	**571**	285.5	190.333	114.2	81.571	51.909
57	3	**581**	290.5	193.666	116.2	83	52.818
58	1	~~591~~	295.5	~~197~~	118.2	84.428	53.727
59	2	**601**	300.5	200.333	120.2	85.857	54.636
60	3	**611**	305.5	203.666	122.2	87.285	55.545
61	1	~~621~~	310.5	~~207~~	124.2	88.714	56.454
62	2	*631*	315.5	210.333	126.2	90.142	57.363
63	3	641	320.5	213.666	128.2	91.571	58.272
64	1	~~651~~	325.5	~~217~~	130.2	93	59.181
65	2	*661*	330.5	220.333	132.2	94.428	60.09
66	3	**671**	335.5	223.666	134.2	95.857	61
67	1	~~681~~	340.5	~~227~~	136.2	97.285	61.909
68	2	*691*	345.5	230.333	138.2	98.714	62.818
69	3	**701**	350.5	233.666	140.2	100.142	63.727
70	1	~~711~~	355.5	~~237~~	142.2	101.571	64.636
71	2	**721**	360.5	240.333	144.2	103	65.545
72	3	**731**	365.5	243.666	146.2	104.428	66.454
73	1	~~741~~	370.5	~~247~~	148.2	105.857	67.363

74	2	751	375.5	250.333	150.2	107.285	68.272
75	3	761	380.5	253.666	152.2	108.714	69.181
76	1	~~771~~	385.5	~~257~~	154.2	110.142	70.09
77	2	781	390.5	260.333	156.2	111.571	71
78	3	791	395.5	263.666	158.2	113	71.909
79	1	~~801~~	400.5	~~267~~	160.2	114.428	72.818
80	2	*811*	405.5	270.333	162.2	115.857	73.727
81	3	821	410.5	273.666	164.2	117.285	74.636
82	1	~~831~~	415.5	~~277~~	166.2	118.714	75.545
83	2	841	420.5	280.333	168.2	120.142	76.454
84	3	851	425.5	283.666	170.2	121.571	77.363
85	1	~~861~~	430.5	~~287~~	172.2	123	78.272
86	2	871	435.5	290.333	174.2	124.428	79.181
87	3	881	440.5	293.666	176.2	125.857	80.09
88	1	~~891~~	445.5	~~297~~	178.2	127.285	81
89	2	901	450.5	300.333	180.2	128.714	81.909
90	3	911	455.5	303.666	182.2	130.142	82.818
91	1	~~921~~	460.5	~~307~~	184.2	131.571	83.727
92	2	931	465.5	310.333	186.2	133	84.636
93	3	941	470.5	313.666	188.2	134.428	85.545
94	1	~~951~~	475.5	~~317~~	190.2	135.857	86.454
95	2	961	480.5	320.333	192.2	137.285	87.363
96	3	971	485.5	323.666	194.2	138.714	88.272
97	1	~~981~~	490.5	~~327~~	196.2	140.142	89.181
98	2	991	495.5	330.333	198.2	141.571	90.09
99	3	1001	500.5	333.666	200.2	143	91
100	1	~~1011~~	505.5	~~337~~	202.2	144.428	91.909
101	2	*1021*	510.5	340.333	204.2	145.857	92.818
102	3	1031	515.5	343.666	206.2	147.285	93.727
103	1	~~1041~~	520.5	~~347~~	208.2	148.714	94.636

104	2	1051	525.5	350.333	210.2	150.142	95.545
105	3	1061	530.5	353.666	212.2	151.571	96.454
106	1	1071	535.5	357	214.2	153	97.363
107	2	1081	540.5	360.333	216.2	154.428	98.272
108	3	1091	545.5	363.666	218.2	155.857	99.181
109	1	1101	550.5	367	220.2	157.285	100.09
110	2	1111	555.5	370.333	222.2	158.714	101
111	3	1121	560.5	373.666	224.2	160.142	101.909
112	1	1131	565.5	377	226.2	161.571	102.818
113	2	1141	570.5	380.333	228.2	163	103.727
114	3	1151	575.5	383.666	230.2	164.428	104.636
115	1	1161	580.5	387	232.2	165.857	105.545
116	2	1171	585.5	390.333	234.2	167.285	106.454
117	3	1181	590.5	393.666	236.2	168.714	107.363
118	1	1191	595.5	397	238.2	170.142	108.272
119	2	1201	600.5	400.333	240.2	171.571	109.181
120	3	1211	605.5	403.666	242.2	173	110.09
121	1	1221	610.5	407	244.2	174.428	111
122	2	1231	615.5	410.333	246.2	175.857	111.909
123	3	1241	620.5	413.666	248.2	177.285	112.818
124	1	1251	625.5	417	250.2	178.714	113.727
125	2	1261	630.5	420.333	252.2	180.142	114.636
126	3	1271	635.5	423.666	254.2	181.571	115.545
127	1	1281	640.5	427	256.2	183	116.454
128	2	1291	645.5	430.333	258.2	184.428	117.363
129	3	1301	650.5	433.666	260.2	185.857	118.272
130	1	1311	655.5	437	262.2	187.285	119.181
131	2	1321	660.5	440.333	264.2	188.714	120.09
132	3	1331	665.5	443.666	266.2	190.142	121
133	1	1341	670.5	447	268.2	191.571	121.909

134	2	1351	675.5	450.333	270.2	193	122.818
135	3	1361	680.5	453.666	272.2	194.428	123.727
136	1	1371	685.5	457	274.2	195.857	124.636
137	2	1381	690.5	460.333	276.2	197.285	125.545
138	3	1391	695.5	463.666	278.2	198.714	126.454
139	1	1401	700.5	467	280.2	200.142	127.363
140	2	1411	705.5	470.333	282.2	201.571	128.272
141	3	1421	710.5	473.666	284.2	203	129.181
142	1	1431	715.5	477	286.2	204.428	130.09
143	2	1441	720.5	480.333	288.2	205.857	131
144	3	1451	725.5	483.666	290.2	207.285	131.909
145	1	1461	730.5	487	292.2	208.714	132.818
146	2	1471	735.5	490.333	294.2	210.142	133.727
147	3	1481	740.5	493.666	296.2	211.571	134.636
148	1	1491	745.5	497	298.2	213	135.545
149	2	1501	750.5	500.333	300.2	214.428	136.454
150	3	1511	755.5	503.666	302.2	215.857	137.363
151	1	1521	760.5	507	304.2	217.285	138.272
152	2	1531	765.5	510.333	306.2	218.714	139.181
153	3	1541	770.5	513.666	308.2	220.142	140.09
154	1	1551	775.5	517	310.2	221.571	141
155	2	1561	780.5	520.333	312.2	223	141.909
156	3	1571	785.5	523.666	314.2	224.428	142.818
157	1	1581	790.5	527	316.2	225.857	143.727
158	2	1591	795.5	530.333	318.2	227.285	144.636
159	3	1601	800.5	533.666	320.2	228.714	145.545
160	1	1611	805.5	537	322.2	230.142	146.454
161	2	1621	810.5	540.333	324.2	231.571	147.363
162	3	1631	815.5	543.666	326.2	233	148.272
163	1	1641	820.5	547	328.2	234.428	149.181

164	2	**1651**	825.5	550.333	330.2	235.857	150.09
165	3	**1661**	830.5	553.666	332.2	237.285	151
166	1	1671	835.5	557	334.2	238.714	151.909
167	2	**1681**	840.5	560.333	336.2	240.142	152.818
168	3	**1691**	845.5	563.666	338.2	241.571	153.727
169	1	1701	850.5	567	340.2	243	154.636
170	2	**1711**	855.5	570.333	342.2	244.428	155.545
171	3	**1721**	860.5	573.666	344.2	245.857	156.454
172	1	1731	865.5	577	346.2	247.285	157.363
173	2	**1741**	870.5	580.333	348.2	248.714	158.272
174	3	**1751**	875.5	583.666	350.2	250.142	159.181
175	1	1761	880.5	587	352.2	251.571	160.09
176	2	**1771**	885.5	590.333	354.2	253	161
177	3	**1781**	890.5	593.666	356.2	254.428	161.909
178	1	1791	895.5	597	358.2	255.857	162.818
179	2	*1801*	900.5	600.333	360.2	257.285	163.727
180	3	*1811*	905.5	603.666	362.2	258.714	164.636
181	1	1821	910.5	607	364.2	260.142	165.545
182	2	*1831*	915.5	610.333	366.2	261.571	166.454
183	3	**1841**	920.5	613.666	368.2	263	167.363
184	1	1851	925.5	617	370.2	264.428	168.272
185	2	**1861**	930.5	620.333	372.2	265.857	169.181
186	3	**1871**	935.5	623.666	374.2	267.285	170.09
187	1	1881	940.5	627	376.2	268.714	171
188	2	**1891**	945.5	630.333	378.2	270.142	171.909
189	3	**1901**	950.5	633.666	380.2	271.571	172.818
190	1	1911	955.5	637	382.2	273	173.727
191	2	**1921**	960.5	640.333	384.2	274.428	174.636
192	3	**1931**	965.5	643.666	386.2	275.857	175.545
193	1	1941	970.5	647	388.2	277.285	176.454

194	2	*1951*	975.5	650.333	390.2	278.714	177.363
195	3	**1961**	980.5	653.666	392.2	280.142	178.272
196	1	1971	985.5	657	394.2	281.571	179.181
197	2	**1981**	990.5	660.333	396.2	283	180.09
198	3	**1991**	995.5	663.666	398.2	284.428	181
199	1	2001	1000.5	667	400.2	285.857	181.909
200	2	2011	1005.5	670.333	402.2	287.285	182.818
201	3	**2021**	1010.5	673.666	404.2	288.714	183.727

Table 7A. Unit primes white spaces column 1 (gray spaces highlighted)

90

Appendix G

Unit Prime White Space Matrix Column 3

(See chapter 8 for white space explanations and how to calculate white open spaces)

(Table 7B)

LINES	ROWS	COLUMN 3	UNIT PRIME WHITE SPACE MATRIX: COLUMN 3 WHOLE NUMBERS OTHER THAN ONE ARE SPACES EXAMPLE: *TABLE CELL* **203** ÷ BY *UNIT CELL* **7** = **29**				
			UNIT 2 COL 3 NO SPACES	UNIT 3 COL 3 GRAY SPACES	UNIT 5 COL 3 NO SPACES	UNIT 7 COL 3 WHITE SPACES	UNIT 11 COL 3 WHITE SPACES
			NO WHITE SPACES 2	REPEATS DOWN EVERY 3	NO WHITE SPACES 5	REPEATS DOWN EVERY 7	REPEATS DOWN EVERY 11
0	3	13	6.5	4.333	2.6	1.857	1.181
1	1	23	11.5	7.666	4.6	3.285	2.09
2	2	33	16.5	11	6.6	4.714	3
3	3	43	21.5	14.333	8.6	6.142	3.909
4	1	53	26.5	17.666	10.6	7.571	4.818
5	2	63	31.5	21	12.6	9	5.727
6	3	73	36.5	24.333	14.6	10.428	6.636
7	1	83	41.5	27.666	16.6	11.857	7.545
8	2	93	46.5	31	18.6	13.285	8.454
9	3	103	51.5	34.333	20.6	14.714	9.363
10	1	*113*	56.5	37.666	22.6	16.142	10.272
11	2	123	61.5	41	24.6	17.571	11.181
12	3	133	66.5	44.333	26.6	19	12.09
13	1	143	71.5	47.666	28.6	20.428	13

14	2	153	76.5	51	30.6	21.857	13.909
15	3	163	81.5	54.333	32.6	23.285	14.818
16	1	173	86.5	57.666	34.6	24.714	15.727
17	2	183	91.5	61	36.6	26.142	16.636
18	3	193	96.5	64.333	38.6	27.571	17.545
19	1	203	101.5	67.666	40.6	29	18.454
20	2	213	106.5	71	42.6	30.428	19.363
21	3	223	111.5	74.333	44.6	31.857	20.272
22	1	233	116.5	77.666	46.6	33.285	21.181
23	2	243	121.5	81	48.6	34.714	22.09
24	3	253	126.5	84.333	50.6	36.142	23
25	1	263	131.5	87.666	52.6	37.571	23.909
26	2	273	136.5	91	54.6	39	24.818
27	3	283	141.5	94.333	56.6	40.428	25.727
28	1	293	146.5	97.666	58.6	41.857	26.636
29	2	303	151.5	101	60.6	43.285	27.545
30	3	313	156.5	104.333	62.6	44.714	28.454
31	1	323	161.5	107.666	64.6	46.142	29.363
32	2	333	166.5	111	66.6	47.571	30.272
33	3	343	171.5	114.333	68.6	49	31.181
34	1	353	176.5	117.666	70.6	50.428	32.09
35	2	363	181.5	121	72.6	51.857	33
36	3	373	186.5	124.333	74.6	53.285	33.909
37	1	383	191.5	127.666	76.6	54.714	34.818
38	2	393	196.5	131	78.6	56.142	35.727
39	3	403	201.5	134.333	80.6	57.571	36.636
40	1	413	206.5	137.666	82.6	59	37.545
41	2	423	211.5	141	84.6	60.428	38.454
42	3	433	216.5	144.333	86.6	61.857	39.363
43	1	443	221.5	147.666	88.6	63.285	40.272

44	2	453	226.5	151	90.6	64.714	41.181
45	3	463	231.5	154.333	92.6	66.142	42.09
46	1	473	236.5	157.666	94.6	67.571	43
47	2	483	241.5	161	96.6	69	43.909
48	3	493	246.5	164.333	98.6	70.428	44.818
49	1	503	251.5	167.666	100.6	71.857	45.727
50	2	513	256.5	171	102.6	73.285	46.636
51	3	523	261.5	174.333	104.6	74.714	47.545
52	1	533	266.5	177.666	106.6	76.142	48.454
53	2	543	271.5	181	108.6	77.571	49.363
54	3	553	276.5	184.333	110.6	79	50.272
55	1	563	281.5	187.666	112.6	80.428	51.181
56	2	573	286.5	191	114.6	81.857	52.09
57	3	583	291.5	194.333	116.6	83.285	53
58	1	593	296.5	197.666	118.6	84.714	53.909
59	2	603	301.5	201	120.6	86.142	54.818
60	3	613	306.5	204.333	122.6	87.571	55.727
61	1	623	311.5	207.666	124.6	89	56.636
62	2	633	316.5	211	126.6	90.428	57.545
63	3	643	321.5	214.333	128.6	91.857	58.454
64	1	653	326.5	217.666	130.6	93.285	59.363
65	2	663	331.5	221	132.6	94.714	60.272
66	3	673	336.5	224.333	134.6	96.142	61.181
67	1	683	341.5	227.666	136.6	97.571	62.09
68	2	693	346.5	231	138.6	99	63
69	3	703	351.5	234.333	140.6	100.428	63.909
70	1	713	356.5	237.666	142.6	101.857	64.818
71	2	723	361.5	241	144.6	103.285	65.727
72	3	733	366.5	244.333	146.6	104.714	66.636
73	1	743	371.5	247.666	148.6	106.142	67.545

74	2	~~753~~	376.5	~~251~~	150.6	107.571	68.454
75	3	763	381.5	254.333	152.6	109	69.363
76	1	_773_	386.5	257.666	154.6	110.428	70.272
77	2	~~783~~	391.5	~~261~~	156.6	111.857	71.181
78	3	793	396.5	264.333	158.6	113.285	72.09
79	1	803	401.5	267.666	160.6	114.714	73
80	2	~~813~~	406.5	~~271~~	162.6	116.142	73.909
81	3	823	411.5	274.333	164.6	117.571	74.818
82	1	833	416.5	277.666	166.6	119	75.727
83	2	~~843~~	421.5	~~281~~	168.6	120.428	76.636
84	3	853	426.5	284.333	170.6	121.857	77.545
85	1	_863_	431.5	287.666	172.6	123.285	78.454
86	2	~~873~~	436.5	~~291~~	174.6	124.714	79.363
87	3	883	441.5	294.333	176.6	126.142	80.272
88	1	893	446.5	297.666	178.6	127.571	81.181
89	2	~~903~~	451.5	~~301~~	180.6	129	82.09
90	3	913	456.5	304.333	182.6	130.428	83
91	1	923	461.5	307.666	184.6	131.857	83.909
92	2	~~933~~	466.5	~~311~~	186.6	133.285	84.818
93	3	943	471.5	314.333	188.6	134.714	85.727
94	1	_953_	476.5	317.666	190.6	136.142	86.636
95	2	~~963~~	481.5	~~321~~	192.6	137.571	87.545
96	3	973	486.5	324.333	194.6	139	88.454
97	1	_983_	491.5	327.666	196.6	140.428	89.363
98	2	~~993~~	496.5	~~331~~	198.6	141.857	90.272
99	3	1003	501.5	334.333	200.6	143.285	91.181
100	1	1013	506.5	337.666	202.6	144.714	92.09
101	2	~~1023~~	511.5	~~341~~	204.6	146.142	93
102	3	1033	516.5	344.333	206.6	147.571	93.909
103	1	1043	521.5	347.666	208.6	149	94.818

104	2	~~1053~~	526.5	~~351~~	210.6	150.428	95.727
105	3	1063	531.5	354.333	212.6	151.857	96.636
106	1	1073	536.5	357.666	214.6	153.285	97.545
107	2	~~1083~~	541.5	~~361~~	216.6	154.714	98.454
108	3	1093	546.5	364.333	218.6	156.142	99.363
109	1	1103	551.5	367.666	220.6	157.571	100.272
110	2	~~1113~~	556.5	~~371~~	222.6	[159]	101.181
111	3	1123	561.5	374.333	224.6	160.428	102.09
112	1	1133	566.5	377.666	226.6	161.857	[103]
113	2	~~1143~~	571.5	~~381~~	228.6	163.285	103.909
114	3	1153	576.5	384.333	230.6	164.714	104.818
115	1	*~~1163~~*	581.5	387.666	232.6	166.142	105.727
116	2	~~1173~~	586.5	~~391~~	234.6	167.571	106.636
117	3	1183	591.5	394.333	236.6	[169]	107.545
118	1	*~~1193~~*	596.5	397.666	238.6	170.428	108.454
119	2	~~1203~~	601.5	~~401~~	240.6	171.857	109.363
120	3	1213	606.5	404.333	242.6	173.285	110.272
121	1	~~1223~~	611.5	407.666	244.6	174.714	111.181
122	2	~~1233~~	616.5	~~411~~	246.6	176.142	112.09
123	3	1243	621.5	414.333	248.6	177.571	[113]
124	1	1253	626.5	417.666	250.6	[179]	113.909
125	2	~~1263~~	631.5	~~421~~	252.6	180.428	114.818
126	3	1273	636.5	424.333	254.6	181.857	115.727
127	1	~~1283~~	641.5	427.666	256.6	183.285	116.636
128	2	~~1293~~	646.5	~~431~~	258.6	184.714	117.545
129	3	1303	651.5	434.333	260.6	186.142	118.454
130	1	1313	656.5	437.666	262.6	187.571	119.363
131	2	~~1323~~	661.5	~~441~~	264.6	[189]	120.272
132	3	1333	666.5	444.333	266.6	190.428	121.181
133	1	1343	671.5	447.666	268.6	191.857	122.09

134	2	1353	676.5	451	270.6	193.285	123
135	3	1363	681.5	454.333	272.6	194.714	123.909
136	1	*1373*	686.5	457.666	274.6	196.142	124.818
137	2	1383	691.5	461	276.6	197.571	125.727
138	3	1393	696.5	464.333	278.6	199	126.636
139	1	1403	701.5	467.666	280.6	200.428	127.545
140	2	1413	706.5	471	282.6	201.857	128.454
141	3	1423	711.5	474.333	284.6	203.285	129.363
142	1	1433	716.5	477.666	286.6	204.714	130.272
143	2	1443	721.5	481	288.6	206.142	131.181
144	3	1453	726.5	484.333	290.6	207.571	132.09
145	1	1463	731.5	487.666	292.6	209	133
146	2	1473	736.5	491	294.6	210.428	133.909
147	3	1483	741.5	494.333	296.6	211.857	134.818
148	1	1493	746.5	497.666	298.6	213.285	135.727
149	2	1503	751.5	501	300.6	214.714	136.636
150	3	1513	756.5	504.333	302.6	216.142	137.545
151	1	*1523*	761.5	507.666	304.6	217.571	138.454
152	2	1533	766.5	511	306.6	219	139.363
153	3	1543	771.5	514.333	308.6	220.428	140.272
154	1	1553	776.5	517.666	310.6	221.857	141.181
155	2	1563	781.5	521	312.6	223.285	142.09
156	3	1573	786.5	524.333	314.6	224.714	143
157	1	*1583*	791.5	527.666	316.6	226.142	143.909
158	2	1593	796.5	531	318.6	227.571	144.818
159	3	1603	801.5	534.333	320.6	229	145.727
160	1	1613	806.5	537.666	322.6	230.428	146.636
161	2	1623	811.5	541	324.6	231.857	147.545
162	3	1633	816.5	544.333	326.6	233.285	148.454
163	1	1643	821.5	547.666	328.6	234.714	149.363

164	2	~~1653~~	826.5	~~551~~	330.6	236.142	150.272
165	3	1663	831.5	554.333	332.6	237.571	151.181
166	1	1673	836.5	557.666	334.6	239	152.09
167	2	~~1683~~	841.5	~~561~~	336.6	240.428	153
168	3	1693	846.5	564.333	338.6	241.857	153.909
169	1	1703	851.5	567.666	340.6	243.285	154.818
170	2	~~1743~~	856.5	~~571~~	342.6	244.714	155.727
171	3	1723	861.5	574.333	344.6	246.142	156.636
172	1	*1733*	866.5	577.666	346.6	247.571	157.545
173	2	~~1743~~	871.5	~~581~~	348.6	249	158.454
174	3	1753	876.5	584.333	350.6	250.428	159.363
175	1	1763	881.5	587.666	352.6	251.857	160.272
176	2	~~1773~~	886.5	~~591~~	354.6	253.285	161.181
177	3	1783	891.5	594.333	356.6	254.714	162.09
178	1	1793	896.5	597.666	358.6	256.142	163
179	2	~~1803~~	901.5	~~601~~	360.6	257.571	163.909
180	3	1813	906.5	604.333	362.6	259	164.818
181	1	*1823*	911.5	607.666	364.6	260.428	165.727
182	2	~~1833~~	916.5	~~611~~	366.6	261.857	166.636
183	3	1843	921.5	614.333	368.6	263.285	167.545
184	1	1853	926.5	617.666	370.6	264.714	168.454
185	2	~~1863~~	931.5	~~621~~	372.6	266.142	169.363
186	3	1873	936.5	624.333	374.6	267.571	170.272
187	1	1883	941.5	627.666	376.6	269	171.181
188	2	~~1893~~	946.5	~~631~~	378.6	270.428	172.09
189	3	1903	951.5	634.333	380.6	271.857	173
190	1	*1913*	956.5	637.666	382.6	273.285	173.909
191	2	~~1923~~	961.5	~~641~~	384.6	274.714	174.818
192	3	1933	966.5	644.333	386.6	276.142	175.727
193	1	1943	971.5	647.666	388.6	277.571	176.636

194	2	1953	976.5	651	390.6	279	177.545
195	3	1963	981.5	654.333	392.6	280.428	178.454
196	1	1973	986.5	657.666	394.6	281.857	179.363
197	2	1983	991.5	661	396.6	283.285	180.272
198	3	1993	996.5	664.333	398.6	284.714	181.181
199	1	2003	1001.5	667.666	400.6	286.142	182.09
200	2	2013	1006.5	671	402.6	287.571	183
201	3	2023	1011.5	674.333	404.6	289	183.909

Table 7B. Unit primes white spaces column 3 (gray spaces highlighted)

Appendix H

Unit Prime White Space Matrix Column 7

(See chapter 8 for white space explanations and how to calculate white open spaces)

(Table 7C)

LINES	ROWS	COLUMN 7	UNIT PRIME WHITE SPACE MATRIX: COLUMN 7 WHOLE NUMBERS OTHER THAN ONE ARE SPACES EXAMPLE: TABLE CELL 187 ÷ BY UNIT CELL 11 = 17				
			UNIT 2 COL 7 NO SPACES	UNIT 3 COL 7 GRAY SPACES	UNIT 5 COL 7 NO SPACES	UNIT 7 COL 7 WHITE SPACES	UNIT 11 COL 7 WHITE SPACES
			NO WHITE SPACES 2	REPEATS DOWN EVERY 3	NO WHITE SPACES 5	REPEATS DOWN EVERY 7	REPEATS DOWN EVERY 11
0	3	17	8.5	5.666	3.4	2.428	1.545
1	1	27	13.5	9	5.4	3.857	2.454
2	2	37	18.5	12.333	7.4	5.285	3.363
3	3	47	23.5	15.666	9.4	6.714	4.272
4	1	57	28.5	19	11.4	8.142	5.181
5	2	67	33.5	22.333	13.4	9.571	6.09
6	3	77	38.5	25.666	15.4	11	7
7	1	87	43.5	29	17.4	12.428	7.909
8	2	97	48.5	32.333	19.4	13.857	8.818
9	3	107	53.5	35.666	21.4	15.285	9.727
10	1	117	58.5	39	23.4	16.714	10.636
11	2	127	63.5	42.333	25.4	18.142	11.545
12	3	137	68.5	45.666	27.4	19.571	12.454
13	1	147	73.5	49	29.4	21	13.363

14	2	157	78.5	52.333	31.4	22.428	14.272
15	3	167	83.5	55.666	33.4	23.857	15.181
16	1	~~177~~	88.5	~~59~~	35.4	25.285	16.09
17	2	187	93.5	62.333	37.4	26.714	17
18	3	197	98.5	65.666	39.4	28.142	17.909
19	1	~~207~~	103.5	~~69~~	41.4	29.571	18.818
20	2	217	108.5	72.333	43.4	31	19.727
21	3	227	113.5	75.666	45.4	32.428	20.636
22	1	~~237~~	118.5	~~79~~	47.4	33.857	21.545
23	2	247	123.5	82.333	49.4	35.285	22.454
24	3	257	128.5	85.666	51.4	36.714	23.363
25	1	~~267~~	133.5	~~89~~	53.4	38.142	24.272
26	2	277	138.5	92.333	55.4	39.571	25.181
27	3	287	143.5	95.666	57.4	41	26.09
28	1	~~297~~	148.5	~~99~~	59.4	42.428	27
29	2	*307*	153.5	102.333	61.4	43.857	27.909
30	3	317	158.5	105.666	63.4	45.285	28.818
31	1	~~327~~	163.5	~~109~~	65.4	46.714	29.727
32	2	337	168.5	112.333	67.4	48.142	30.636
33	3	347	173.5	115.666	69.4	49.571	31.545
34	1	~~357~~	178.5	~~119~~	71.4	51	32.454
35	2	*367*	183.5	122.333	73.4	52.428	33.363
36	3	377	188.5	125.666	75.4	53.857	34.272
37	1	~~387~~	193.5	~~129~~	77.4	55.285	35.181
38	2	*397*	198.5	132.333	79.4	56.714	36.09
39	3	407	203.5	135.666	81.4	58.142	37
40	1	~~417~~	208.5	~~139~~	83.4	59.571	37.909
41	2	427	213.5	142.333	85.4	61	38.818
42	3	437	218.5	145.666	87.4	62.428	39.727
43	1	~~447~~	223.5	~~149~~	89.4	63.857	40.636

44	2	*457*	228.5	152.333	91.4	65.285	41.545
45	3	467	233.5	155.666	93.4	66.714	42.454
46	1	477	238.5	159	95.4	68.142	43.363
47	2	*487*	243.5	162.333	97.4	69.571	44.272
48	3	497	248.5	165.666	99.4	71	45.181
49	1	507	253.5	169	101.4	72.428	46.09
50	2	517	258.5	172.333	103.4	73.857	47
51	3	527	263.5	175.666	105.4	75.285	47.909
52	1	537	268.5	179	107.4	76.714	48.818
53	2	547	273.5	182.333	109.4	78.142	49.727
54	3	*557*	278.5	185.666	111.4	79.571	50.636
55	1	567	283.5	189	113.4	81	51.545
56	2	577	288.5	192.333	115.4	82.428	52.454
57	3	*587*	293.5	195.666	117.4	83.857	53.363
58	1	597	298.5	199	119.4	85.285	54.272
59	2	607	303.5	202.333	121.4	86.714	55.181
60	3	617	308.5	205.666	123.4	88.142	56.09
61	1	627	313.5	209	125.4	89.571	57
62	2	637	318.5	212.333	127.4	91	57.909
63	3	647	323.5	215.666	129.4	92.428	58.818
64	1	657	328.5	219	131.4	93.857	59.727
65	2	667	333.5	222.333	133.4	95.285	60.636
66	3	677	338.5	225.666	135.4	96.714	61.545
67	1	687	343.5	229	137.4	98.142	62.454
68	2	697	348.5	232.333	139.4	99.571	63.363
69	3	707	353.5	235.666	141.4	101	64.272
70	1	717	358.5	239	143.4	102.428	65.181
71	2	*727*	363.5	242.333	145.4	103.857	66.09
72	3	737	368.5	245.666	147.4	105.285	67
73	1	747	373.5	249	149.4	106.714	67.909

74	2	757	378.5	252.333	151.4	108.142	68.818
75	3	767	383.5	255.666	153.4	109.571	69.727
76	1	777	388.5	259	155.4	111	70.636
77	2	787	393.5	262.333	157.4	112.428	71.545
78	3	797	398.5	265.666	159.4	113.857	72.454
79	1	807	403.5	269	161.4	115.285	73.363
80	2	817	408.5	272.333	163.4	116.714	74.272
81	3	827	413.5	275.666	165.4	118.142	75.181
82	1	837	418.5	279	167.4	119.571	76.09
83	2	847	423.5	282.333	169.4	121	77
84	3	857	428.5	285.666	171.4	122.428	77.909
85	1	867	433.5	289	173.4	123.857	78.818
86	2	877	438.5	292.333	175.4	125.285	79.727
87	3	887	443.5	295.666	177.4	126.714	80.636
88	1	897	448.5	299	179.4	128.142	81.545
89	2	907	453.5	302.333	181.4	129.571	82.454
90	3	917	458.5	305.666	183.4	131	83.363
91	1	927	463.5	309	185.4	132.428	84.272
92	2	937	468.5	312.333	187.4	133.857	85.181
93	3	947	473.5	315.666	189.4	135.285	86.09
94	1	957	478.5	319	191.4	136.714	87
95	2	967	483.5	322.333	193.4	138.142	87.909
96	3	977	488.5	325.666	195.4	139.571	88.818
97	1	987	493.5	329	197.4	141	89.727
98	2	997	498.5	332.333	199.4	142.428	90.636
99	3	1007	503.5	335.666	201.4	143.857	91.545
100	1	1017	508.5	339	203.4	145.285	92.454
101	2	1027	513.5	342.333	205.4	146.714	93.363
102	3	1037	518.5	345.666	207.4	148.142	94.272
103	1	1047	523.5	349	209.4	149.571	95.181

104	2	**1057**	528.5	352.333	211.4	151	96.09
105	3	**1067**	533.5	355.666	213.4	152.428	97
106	1	~~1077~~	538.5	~~359~~	215.4	153.857	97.909
107	2	*1087*	543.5	362.333	217.4	155.285	98.818
108	3	**1097**	548.5	365.666	219.4	156.714	99.727
109	1	~~1107~~	553.5	~~369~~	221.4	158.142	100.636
110	2	*1117*	558.5	372.333	223.4	159.571	101.545
111	3	**1127**	563.5	375.666	225.4	161	102.454
112	1	~~1137~~	568.5	~~379~~	227.4	162.428	103.363
113	2	**1147**	573.5	382.333	229.4	163.857	104.272
114	3	**1157**	578.5	385.666	231.4	165.285	105.181
115	1	~~1167~~	583.5	~~389~~	233.4	166.714	106.09
116	2	**1177**	588.5	392.333	235.4	168.142	107
117	3	**1187**	593.5	395.666	237.4	169.571	107.909
118	1	~~1197~~	598.5	~~399~~	239.4	171	108.818
119	2	**1207**	603.5	402.333	241.4	172.428	109.727
120	3	**1217**	608.5	405.666	243.4	173.857	110.636
121	1	~~1227~~	613.5	~~409~~	245.4	175.285	111.545
122	2	**1237**	618.5	412.333	247.4	176.714	112.454
123	3	**1247**	623.5	415.666	249.4	178.142	113.363
124	1	~~1257~~	628.5	~~419~~	251.4	179.571	114.272
125	2	**1267**	633.5	422.333	253.4	181	115.181
126	3	**1277**	638.5	425.666	255.4	182.428	116.09
127	1	~~1287~~	643.5	~~429~~	257.4	183.857	117
128	2	**1297**	648.5	432.333	259.4	185.285	117.909
129	3	**1307**	653.5	435.666	261.4	186.714	118.818
130	1	~~1317~~	658.5	~~439~~	263.4	188.142	119.727
131	2	**1327**	663.5	442.333	265.4	189.571	120.636
132	3	**1337**	668.5	445.666	267.4	191	121.545
133	1	~~1347~~	673.5	~~449~~	269.4	192.428	122.454

134	2	1357	678.5	452.333	271.4	193.857	123.363
135	3	1367	683.5	455.666	273.4	195.285	124.272
136	1	1377	688.5	459	275.4	196.714	125.181
137	2	1387	693.5	462.333	277.4	198.142	126.09
138	3	1397	698.5	465.666	279.4	199.571	127
139	1	1407	703.5	469	281.4	201	127.909
140	2	1417	708.5	472.333	283.4	202.428	128.818
141	3	1427	713.5	475.666	285.4	203.857	129.727
142	1	1437	718.5	479	287.4	205.285	130.636
143	2	1447	723.5	482.333	289.4	206.714	131.545
144	3	1457	728.5	485.666	291.4	208.142	132.454
145	1	1467	733.5	489	293.4	209.571	133.363
146	2	1477	738.5	492.333	295.4	211	134.272
147	3	1487	743.5	495.666	297.4	212.428	135.181
148	1	1497	748.5	499	299.4	213.857	136.09
149	2	1507	753.5	502.333	301.4	215.285	137
150	3	1517	758.5	505.666	303.4	216.714	137.909
151	1	1527	763.5	509	305.4	218.142	138.818
152	2	1537	768.5	512.333	307.4	219.571	139.727
153	3	1547	773.5	515.666	309.4	221	140.636
154	1	1557	778.5	519	311.4	222.428	141.545
155	2	1567	783.5	522.333	313.4	223.857	142.454
156	3	1577	788.5	525.666	315.4	225.285	143.363
157	1	1587	793.5	529	317.4	226.714	144.272
158	2	1597	798.5	532.333	319.4	228.142	145.181
159	3	1607	803.5	535.666	321.4	229.571	146.09
160	1	1617	808.5	539	323.4	231	147
161	2	1627	813.5	542.333	325.4	232.428	147.909
162	3	1637	818.5	545.666	327.4	233.857	148.818
163	1	1647	823.5	549	329.4	235.285	149.727

164	2	*1657*	828.5	552.333	331.4	236.714	150.636
165	3	1667	833.5	555.666	333.4	238.142	151.545
166	1	1677	838.5	559	335.4	239.571	152.454
167	2	1687	843.5	562.333	337.4	241	153.363
168	3	1697	848.5	565.666	339.4	242.428	154.272
169	1	1707	853.5	569	341.4	243.857	155.181
170	2	1717	858.5	572.333	343.4	245.285	156.09
171	3	1727	863.5	575.666	345.4	246.714	157
172	1	1737	868.5	579	347.4	248.142	157.909
173	2	1747	873.5	582.333	349.4	249.571	158.818
174	3	1757	878.5	585.666	351.4	251	159.727
175	1	1767	883.5	589	353.4	252.428	160.636
176	2	*1777*	888.5	592.333	355.4	253.857	161.545
177	3	1787	893.5	595.666	357.4	255.285	162.454
178	1	1797	898.5	599	359.4	256.714	163.363
179	2	1807	903.5	602.333	361.4	258.142	164.272
180	3	1817	908.5	605.666	363.4	259.571	165.181
181	1	1827	913.5	609	365.4	261	166.09
182	2	1837	918.5	612.333	367.4	262.428	167
183	3	*1847*	923.5	615.666	369.4	263.857	167.909
184	1	1857	928.5	619	371.4	265.285	168.818
185	2	1867	933.5	622.333	373.4	266.714	169.727
186	3	1877	938.5	625.666	375.4	268.142	170.636
187	1	1887	943.5	629	377.4	269.571	171.545
188	2	1897	948.5	632.333	379.4	271	172.454
189	3	1907	953.5	635.666	381.4	272.428	173.363
190	1	1917	958.5	639	383.4	273.857	174.272
191	2	1927	963.5	642.333	385.4	275.285	175.181
192	3	1937	968.5	645.666	387.4	276.714	176.09
193	1	1947	973.5	649	389.4	278.142	177

194	2	**1957**	978.5	652.333	391.4	279.571	177.909
195	3	**1967**	983.5	655.666	393.4	281	178.818
196	1	~~1977~~	988.5	~~659~~	395.4	282.428	179.727
197	2	*1987*	993.5	662.333	397.4	283.857	180.636
198	3	**1997**	998.5	665.666	399.4	285.285	181.545
199	1	~~2007~~	1003.5	~~669~~	401.4	286.714	182.454
200	2	2017	1008.5	672.333	403.4	288.142	183.363
201	3	2027	1013.5	675.666	405.4	289.571	184.272

Table 7C. Unit primes white spaces column 7 (gray spaces highlighted)

Appendix I

Unit Prime White Space Matrix Column 9

(See chapter 8 for white space explanations and how to calculate white open spaces)

(Table 7D)

LINES	ROWS	COLUMN 9	UNIT PRIME WHITE SPACE MATRIX: COLUMN 9 WHOLE NUMBERS OTHER THAN ONE ARE SPACES EXAMPLE: TABLE CELL 169 ÷ BY UNIT CELL 13 = 13				
			UNIT 2 COL 9 NO SPACES	UNIT 3 COL 9 GRAY SPACES	UNIT 5 COL 9 NO SPACES	UNIT 7 COL 9 WHITE SPACES	UNIT 11 COL 9 WHITE SPACES
			NO WHITE SPACES 2	REPEATS DOWN EVERY 3	NO WHITE SPACES 5	REPEATS DOWN EVERY 7	REPEATS DOWN EVERY 11
0	3	19	9.5	6.333	3.8	2.714	1.727
1	1	29	14.5	9.666	5.8	4.142	2.636
2	2	39	19.5	13	7.8	5.571	3.545
3	3	49	24.5	16.333	9.8	7	4.454
4	1	59	29.5	19.666	11.8	8.428	5.363
5	2	69	34.5	23	13.8	9.857	6.272
6	3	79	39.5	26.333	15.8	11.285	7.181
7	1	89	44.5	29.666	17.8	12.714	8.09
8	2	99	49.5	33	19.8	14.142	9
9	3	109	54.5	36.333	21.8	15.571	9.909
10	1	119	59.5	39.666	23.8	17	10.818
`11	2	129	64.5	43	25.8	18.428	11.727
12	3	139	69.5	46.333	27.8	19.857	12.636
13	1	149	74.5	49.666	29.8	21.285	13.545

14	2	~~159~~	79.5	~~53~~	31.8	22.714	14.454
15	3	169	84.5	56.333	33.8	24.142	15.363
16	1	179	89.5	59.666	35.8	25.571	16.272
17	2	~~189~~	94.5	~~63~~	37.8	27	17.181
18	3	199	99.5	66.333	39.8	28.428	18.09
19	1	209	104.5	69.666	41.8	29.857	19
20	2	~~219~~	109.5	~~73~~	43.8	31.285	19.909
21	3	229	114.5	76.333	45.8	32.714	20.818
22	1	239	119.5	79.666	47.8	34.142	21.727
23	2	~~249~~	124.5	~~83~~	49.8	35.571	22.636
24	3	259	129.5	86.333	51.8	37	23.545
25	1	269	134.5	89.666	53.8	38.428	24.454
26	2	~~279~~	139.5	~~93~~	55.8	39.857	25.363
27	3	289	144.5	96.333	57.8	41.285	26.272
28	1	299	149.5	99.666	59.8	42.714	27.181
29	2	~~309~~	154.5	~~103~~	61.8	44.142	28.09
30	3	319	159.5	106.333	63.8	45.571	29
31	1	329	164.5	109.666	65.8	47	29.909
32	2	~~339~~	169.5	~~113~~	67.8	48.428	30.818
33	3	349	174.5	116.333	69.8	49.857	31.727
34	1	359	179.5	119.666	71.8	51.285	32.636
35	2	~~369~~	184.5	~~123~~	73.8	52.714	33.545
36	3	379	189.5	126.333	75.8	54.142	34.454
37	1	389	194.5	129.666	77.8	55.571	35.363
38	2	~~399~~	199.5	~~133~~	79.8	57	36.272
39	3	409	204.5	136.333	81.8	58.428	37.181
40	1	*419*	209.5	139.666	83.8	59.857	38.09
41	2	~~429~~	214.5	~~143~~	85.8	61.285	39
42	3	439	219.5	146.333	87.8	62.714	39.909
43	1	449	224.5	149.666	89.8	64.142	40.818

44	2	~~459~~	229.5	~~153~~	91.8	65.571	41.727
45	3	469	234.5	156.333	93.8	67	42.636
46	1	_479_	239.5	159.666	95.8	68.428	43.545
47	2	~~489~~	244.5	~~163~~	97.8	69.857	44.454
48	3	499	249.5	166.333	99.8	71.285	45.363
49	1	509	254.5	169.666	101.8	72.714	46.272
50	2	~~519~~	259.5	~~173~~	103.8	74.142	47.181
51	3	529	264.5	176.333	105.8	75.571	48.09
52	1	539	269.5	179.666	107.8	77	49
53	2	~~549~~	274.5	~~183~~	109.8	78.428	49.909
54	3	559	279.5	186.333	111.8	79.857	50.818
55	1	569	284.5	189.666	113.8	81.285	51.727
56	2	~~579~~	289.5	~~193~~	115.8	82.714	52.636
57	3	589	294.5	196.333	117.8	84.142	53.545
58	1	599	299.5	199.666	119.8	85.571	54.454
59	2	~~609~~	304.5	~~203~~	121.8	87	55.363
60	3	619	309.5	206.333	123.8	88.428	56.272
61	1	629	314.5	209.666	125.8	89.857	57.181
62	2	~~639~~	319.5	~~213~~	127.8	91.285	58.09
63	3	649	324.5	216.333	129.8	92.714	59
64	1	659	329.5	219.666	131.8	94.142	59.909
65	2	~~669~~	334.5	~~223~~	133.8	95.571	60.818
66	3	679	339.5	226.333	135.8	97	61.727
67	1	689	344.5	229.666	137.8	98.428	62.636
68	2	~~699~~	349.5	~~233~~	139.8	99.857	63.545
69	3	709	354.5	236.333	141.8	101.285	64.454
70	1	_719_	359.5	239.666	143.8	102.714	65.363
71	2	~~729~~	364.5	~~243~~	145.8	104.142	66.272
72	3	739	369.5	246.333	147.8	105.571	67.181
73	1	749	374.5	249.666	149.8	107	68.09

74	2	~~759~~	379.5	~~253~~	151.8	108.428	69
75	3	769	384.5	256.333	153.8	109.857	69.909
76	1	779	389.5	259.666	155.8	111.285	70.818
77	2	~~789~~	394.5	~~263~~	157.8	112.714	71.727
78	3	799	399.5	266.333	159.8	114.142	72.636
79	1	*809*	404.5	269.666	161.8	115.571	73.545
80	2	~~819~~	409.5	~~273~~	163.8	117	74.454
81	3	829	414.5	276.333	165.8	118.428	75.363
82	1	*839*	419.5	279.666	167.8	119.857	76.272
83	2	~~849~~	424.5	~~283~~	169.8	121.285	77.181
84	3	859	429.5	286.333	171.8	122.714	78.09
85	1	869	434.5	289.666	173.8	124.142	79
86	2	~~879~~	439.5	~~293~~	175.8	125.571	79.909
87	3	889	444.5	296.333	177.8	127	80.818
88	1	899	449.5	299.666	179.8	128.428	81.727
89	2	~~909~~	454.5	~~303~~	181.8	129.857	82.636
90	3	919	459.5	306.333	183.8	131.285	83.545
91	1	*929*	464.5	309.666	185.8	132.714	84.454
92	2	~~939~~	469.5	~~313~~	187.8	134.142	85.363
93	3	949	474.5	316.333	189.8	135.571	86.272
94	1	959	479.5	319.666	191.8	137	87.181
95	2	~~969~~	484.5	~~323~~	193.8	138.428	88.09
96	3	979	489.5	326.333	195.8	139.857	89
97	1	989	494.5	329.666	197.8	141.285	89.909
98	2	~~999~~	499.5	~~333~~	199.8	142.714	90.818
99	3	*1009*	504.5	336.333	201.8	144.142	91.727
100	1	1019	509.5	339.666	203.8	145.571	92.636
101	2	~~1029~~	514.5	~~343~~	205.8	147	93.545
102	3	1039	519.5	346.333	207.8	148.428	94.454
103	1	*1049*	524.5	349.666	209.8	149.857	95.363

104	2	1059	529.5	353	211.8	151.285	96.272
105	3	1069	534.5	356.333	213.8	152.714	97.181
106	1	1079	539.5	359.666	215.8	154.142	98.09
107	2	1089	544.5	363	217.8	155.571	99
108	3	1099	549.5	366.333	219.8	157	99.909
109	1	1109	554.5	369.666	221.8	158.428	100.818
110	2	1119	559.5	373	223.8	159.857	101.727
111	3	1129	564.5	376.333	225.8	161.285	102.636
112	1	1139	569.5	379.666	227.8	162.714	103.545
113	2	1149	574.5	383	229.8	164.142	104.454
114	3	1159	579.5	386.333	231.8	165.571	105.363
115	1	1169	584.5	389.666	233.8	167	106.272
116	2	1179	589.5	393	235.8	168.428	107.181
117	3	1189	594.5	396.333	237.8	169.857	108.09
118	1	1199	599.5	399.666	239.8	171.285	109
119	2	1209	604.5	403	241.8	172.714	109.909
120	3	1219	609.5	406.333	243.8	174.142	110.818
121	1	1229	614.5	409.666	245.8	175.571	111.727
122	2	1239	619.5	413	247.8	177	112.636
123	3	1249	624.5	416.333	249.8	178.428	113.545
124	1	1259	629.5	419.666	251.8	179.857	114.454
125	2	1269	634.5	423	253.8	181.285	115.363
126	3	1279	639.5	426.333	255.8	182.714	116.272
127	1	1289	644.5	429.666	257.8	184.142	117.181
128	2	1299	649.5	433	259.8	185.571	118.09
129	3	1309	654.5	436.333	261.8	187	119
130	1	1319	659.5	439.666	263.8	188.428	119.909
131	2	1329	664.5	443	265.8	189.857	120.818
132	3	1339	669.5	446.333	267.8	191.285	121.727
133	1	1349	674.5	449.666	269.8	192.714	122.636

134	2	~~1359~~	679.5	~~453~~	271.8	194.142	123.545
135	3	1369	684.5	456.333	273.8	195.571	124.454
136	1	1379	689.5	459.666	275.8	197	125.363
137	2	~~1389~~	694.5	~~463~~	277.8	198.428	126.272
138	3	*1399*	699.5	466.333	279.8	199.857	127.181
139	1	*1409*	704.5	469.666	281.8	201.285	128.09
140	2	~~1419~~	709.5	~~473~~	283.8	202.714	129
141	3	1429	714.5	476.333	285.8	204.142	129.909
142	1	1439	719.5	479.666	287.8	205.571	130.818
143	2	~~1449~~	724.5	~~483~~	289.8	207	131.727
144	3	1459	729.5	486.333	291.8	208.428	132.636
145	1	1469	734.5	489.666	293.8	209.857	133.545
146	2	~~1479~~	739.5	~~493~~	295.8	211.285	134.454
147	3	1489	744.5	496.333	297.8	212.714	135.363
148	1	1499	749.5	499.666	299.8	214.142	136.272
149	2	~~1509~~	754.5	~~503~~	301.8	215.571	137.181
150	3	1519	759.5	506.333	303.8	217	138.09
151	1	1529	764.5	509.666	305.8	218.428	139
152	2	~~1539~~	769.5	~~513~~	307.8	219.857	139.909
153	3	1549	774.5	516.333	309.8	221.285	140.818
154	1	1559	779.5	519.666	311.8	222.714	141.727
155	2	~~1569~~	784.5	~~523~~	313.8	224.142	142.636
156	3	1579	789.5	526.333	315.8	225.571	143.545
157	1	1589	794.5	529.666	317.8	227	144.454
158	2	~~1599~~	799.5	~~533~~	319.8	228.428	145.363
159	3	1609	804.5	536.333	321.8	229.857	146.272
160	1	1619	809.5	539.666	323.8	231.285	147.181
161	2	~~1629~~	814.5	~~543~~	325.8	232.714	148.09
162	3	1639	819.5	546.333	327.8	234.142	149
163	1	1649	824.5	549.666	329.8	235.571	149.909

164	2	~~1659~~	829.5	~~553~~	331.8	237	150.818
165	3	1669	834.5	556.333	333.8	238.428	151.727
166	1	1679	839.5	559.666	335.8	239.857	152.636
167	2	~~1689~~	844.5	~~563~~	337.8	241.285	153.545
168	3	1699	849.5	566.333	339.8	242.714	154.454
169	1	*1709*	854.5	569.666	341.8	244.142	155.363
170	2	~~1719~~	859.5	~~573~~	343.8	245.571	156.272
171	3	1729	864.5	576.333	345.8	247	157.181
172	1	1739	869.5	579.666	347.8	248.428	158.09
173	2	~~1749~~	874.5	~~583~~	349.8	249.857	159
174	3	~~1759~~	879.5	586.333	351.8	251.285	159.909
175	1	1769	884.5	589.666	353.8	252.714	160.818
176	2	~~1779~~	889.5	~~593~~	355.8	254.142	161.727
177	3	1789	894.5	596.333	357.8	255.571	162.636
178	1	1799	899.5	599.666	359.8	257	163.545
179	2	~~1809~~	904.5	~~603~~	361.8	258.428	164.454
180	3	1819	909.5	606.333	363.8	259.857	165.363
181	1	1829	914.5	609.666	365.8	261.285	166.272
182	2	~~1839~~	919.5	~~613~~	367.8	262.714	167.181
183	3	1849	924.5	616.333	369.8	264.142	168.09
184	1	1859	929.5	619.666	371.8	265.571	169
185	2	~~1869~~	934.5	~~623~~	373.8	267	169.909
186	3	1879	939.5	626.333	375.8	268.428	170.818
187	1	*1889*	944.5	629.666	377.8	269.857	171.727
188	2	~~1899~~	949.5	~~633~~	379.8	271.285	172.636
189	3	1909	954.5	636.333	381.8	272.714	173.545
190	1	1919	959.5	639.666	383.8	274.142	174.454
191	2	~~1929~~	964.5	~~643~~	385.8	275.571	175.363
192	3	1939	969.5	646.333	387.8	277	176.272
193	1	*1949*	974.5	649.666	389.8	278.428	177.181

194	2	~~1959~~	979.5	~~653~~	391.8	279.857	178.09
195	3	1969	984.5	656.333	393.8	281.285	179
196	1	1979	989.5	659.666	395.8	282.714	179.909
197	2	~~1989~~	994.5	~~663~~	397.8	284.142	180.818
198	3	1999	999.5	666.333	399.8	285.571	181.727
199	1	2009	1004.5	669.666	401.8	287	182.636
200	2	~~2019~~	1009.5	~~673~~	403.8	288.428	183.545
201	3	2029	1014.5	676.333	405.8	289.857	184.454

Table 7D. Unit primes white spaces column 9 (gray spaces highlighted)

Appendix J

Additional Prime Numbers Proof from
982,433,031 to 982,433,399

(Extended Proof Table 8)

Line	Sequence	Column 1	Column 3	Column 7	Column 9	Alt.
98,243,302	1	982433031	*982433033*	982433037	982433039	
98,243,303	2	982433041	982433043	982433047	982433049	
98,243,304	3	982433051	982433053	982433057	982433059	
98,243,305	1	982433061	982433063	982433067	982433069	
98,243,306	2	982433071	982433073	982433077	982433079	
98,243,307	3	982433081	982433083	982433087	982433089	
98,243,308	1	982433091	982433093	982433097	982433099	
98,243,309	2	982433101	982433103	*982433107*	982433109	
98,243,310	3	982433111	982433113	*982433117*	982433119	2
98,243,311	1	982433121	982433123	982433127	982433129	
98,243,312	2	982433131	982433133	982433137	982433139	
98,243,313	3	982433141	982433143	982433147	982433149	&
98,243,314	1	982433151	982433153	982433157	982433159	
98,243,315	2	982433161	982433163	*982433167*	982433169	
98,243,316	3	982433171	*982433173*	982433177	982433179	1
98,243,317	1	982433181	982433183	982433187	*982433189*	
98,243,318	2	982433191	982433193	982433197	982433199	
98,243,319	3	982433201	982433203	982433207	982433209	
98,243,320	1	982433211	982433213	982433217	*982433219*	
98,243,321	2	982433221	982433223	*982433227*	982433229	
98,243,322	3	982433231	982433233	982433237	982433239	

115

98,243,323	1	982433241	982433243	982433247	982433249	
98,243,324	2	982433251	982433253	982433257	982433259	
98,243,325	3	982433261	982433263	982433267	982433269	
98,243,326	1	982433271	982433273	982433277	_982433279_	
98,243,327	2	982433281	982433283	982433287	982433289	
98,243,328	3	982433291	982433293	982433297	982433299	
98,243,329	1	982433301	982433303	982433307	982433309	
98,243,330	2	982433311	982433313	982433317	982433319	
98,243,331	3	982433321	982433323	982433327	982433329	
98,243,332	1	982433331	982433333	982433337	982433339	
98,243,333	2	982433341	982433343	982433347	982433349	
98,243,334	3	982433351	982433353	982433357	982433359	
98,243,335	1	982433361	982433363	982433367	982433369	
98,243,336	2	982433371	982433373	982433377	982433379	
98,243,337	3	_982433381_	982433383	982433387	982433389	2
98,243,338	1	982433391	982433393	982433397	982433399	

Table 8. Primes at approximately 982 billion

We can see that prime numbers thin out with fewer associations and pair primes, with most primes as red singles. The composites outnumber the primes this far out, as we see most of the spaces are gray or white.